Constructive Virtues
Topics to Avoid in Impolite Company

I0407468

David Satterlee

Praise for David Satterlee and
Constructive Virtues

"[His writing is] humorous, bold and adventurous all at once … channeled through a facility for language and the music of words."

"David isn't afraid of religion, politics or self-inquiry. He is variously father, teacher, friend, inquisitor and voice crying out in the wilderness. He discusses, lectures and rants, but always in a conversational adult voice.

"Somehow both an agnostic and true believer, he radiates optimism — still seeking illumination in dark places. His favorite themes are community, virtues, values and growth. He will tease you into his world and then send you off to explore your own."

Constructive Virtues:

Topics to Avoid in Impolite Company

Essays by David Satterlee

*Further explorations of the important things in life
as individuals, families, communities and societies.*

Dedicated to:
Dianna and the critters
They know where to find me …
and how to bring me back.

This is David Satterlee's second book of collected essays (after *Chum for Thought: Throwing Ideas into Dangerous Waters*). Most of these essays examine values, virtues and ideas that are important to living together well in our developing societies. These values are often denounced out-of-hand by those who cling to old ideas that no longer serve the needs of a changing world.

Follow online at:

DavidSatterlee.blogspot.com
@DavidSatterlee
@ChumForThought
SocioDynamics.org
facebook.com/david.satterlee

First Wordsmith Services trade paperback edition
October 2014

Print ISBN-13: 978-1501063565
Print ISBN-10: 1501063561
ePub ISBN: 978-1310660184

CreateSpace Independent Publishing Platform

Table of Contents

The Path to "Constructive Virtues"

My first published essays were as installments in my newspaper column "@ChumForThought," published in the *Dayton Review*. "Chum" is the word for chopped fish waste that is thrown overboard to attract other fish – especially sharks. I believe that comparing ideas can be a force for good that attracts us to each other. Strangers often become friends as they talk and work together, uniting to solve mutual problems.

The column was intended for my neighbors in a small, rural, Iowa town. I hoped to encourage conservatives to think about their ideas and liberals to come out of the closet. This book, *Constructive Virtues*, extends my collected essays – largely on similar, and sometimes contentious, themes.

Many people prefer to avoid controversy as they would avoid swimming with sharks. You sometimes hear friends say, "I'll talk about anything but politics and religion." I can understand their reluctance and, if a friend tells me that, I'll be the first one to back off and respect his or her need for comfortable beliefs without challenge or doubt.

However, as Proverbs 27:17 says, "As iron sharpens iron, so one man sharpens another." I think it is good to compare notes and discuss ideas. We make both our companions and ourselves better for the time we spend trying to understand each other.

If we withdraw and refuse to talk, empathize, think or compromise with each other, we denounce our brotherhood. People who can't talk together become suspicious and divided. They become fearful and hateful. They become enemies. They often resort to combat to resolve their differences. Unthinking alienation is not the path to peace, security and common good.

Too many people are too ready to, out of hand, disparage and denounce beliefs held by groups other than their own. They forget that other groups' sincere beliefs exist because they are believed to be virtuous! This realization should automatically give pause for thought. Refusing to consider another's worldview damages our potential for understanding, intellectual growth and psychosocial development. Ignorance is rarely considered a noble virtue. How can anyone consider that ignorantly rejecting another's beliefs, values and virtues might be a good thing?

It is often pointed out that gossip, by only discussing *people*, can be damaging. It can useful to know what is going on and discuss *events*. However, I believe that we become better people when we choose to compare and discuss *ideas*.

The ability to communicate about issues, including our values, is what draws us together as friends, families and communities. When we can communicate, we can work together to solve problems; we can unite for common goals and for our common good.

First, a Little Catching-up

After completing *Chum for Thought: Throwing Ideas into Dangerous Waters* (2013), I set out to organize and back-up my writing files. I needed to get a handle on the usual collage of duplicates and versions. In the process, I rediscovered some beloved old friends that still give me "that icy tingle up and down my spine." I've finally given some of these prodigal essays a home.

My father died since publishing my first book of essays. I've produced two writings about him. The first, "Remembering my Dad" was sized to appear as one of my columns in the *Dayton Review*. It leads off — right after this. The final essay, "How I Got from There to Here," is also autobiographical.

"Honoring My Father," is a natural companion piece that I have decided to not duplicate here. It is a memorium to the goodness in Dad's life and an ironic take on the circumstances of a dysfunctional funeral. You can find it separately as its own small book. Naturally, I think it is a good read and recommend it to you.

Remembering my Dad

My father, William (Bill) Satterlee, was 90 years old when he died last week. [January 13, 2013] He started having "spells" and was hospitalized just before Christmas in the southern Missouri town where one of my brothers and his clan live. Dad's body and mind started shutting down and he never recovered.

I made a point of visiting him in the hospital that first week. It turned out that I was able to share some of his last lucid hours. I arrived in the early evening, shortly after the others had left for the day. I helped him finish eating his supper. We enjoyed several hours of sharing stories and catching up on news. The nurses made up a foldout chair and I stayed with him for the night. I fed Dad breakfast in the morning. He told me how to dilute his Cream of Wheat with milk just right so that I could hold it up while he drank it through a straw.

Bill worked hard and played hard too. He was a quiet and modest man, but his eyes could sparkle with mischief before pulling a surprise. He worked on a railroad bridge crew before going to prison in Fort Leavenworth during World War II as a conscientious objector. Dad married his parole officer's oldest daughter when he was 30 and quietly devoted his life to our comfort and security. He worked on a Ford assembly line until he was 67 and his late "surprise baby," our little sister, was married.

I remember watching Dad build our home in Kansas City in the 1950s. He arranged to demolish and remove two older houses and keep the materials. I have vivid memories of watching him pound nails straight and sort them into glass jars. He only owned a trim saw and would cut partway through a 2x4 and turn it over to finish the cut. When he installed hardwood floors in the upstairs bedrooms, he put three finish nails into each joist crossing and explained that, he meant it to last. The house is still the best on that block.

Despite having left school in 8th grade, Bill just seemed to know how to "do stuff" and was generous with his skills. I once overheard two

Elders discussing assignments for construction of a new worship house. They wanted Brother Satterlee to do the trim because "when Bill cuts it, it fits." Dad often took me with him to do volunteer fix-it work – especially for the needy in our congregation. But, while Dad lived a life of brotherhood and faithfulness, he preferred to exercise his spirituality more than to preach it.

Dad loved to travel. He bragged that he had driven on every highway in Colorado. Bill also drove in all 50 states and made twenty-three driving trips from Missouri to Los Angeles, where many relatives had settled. He would plan for two years, anticipating his next big vacation, and then indulge us in adventures such as whitewater rafting and deep-canyon camping.

Dad was never over-proud of his deeds nor over-embarrassed by his indulgences. I recently heard the story that, when Bill was young, his mother told him to eat all of his food before he could have his slice of cherry pie. He told her, "I want to hurry and grow up so that I can eat my pie first." This explains a lot about his fondness for pie and why he sometimes ate dessert first. Dad made all of life as sweet as he could for himself, his family and anyone else he knew. My wife and I went out after his service and had cherry pie before supper in his honor.

Speech: Superman is a Liberal

In the United States, there are two major political parties that spring from two very different general inclinations. Both of these dispositions offer some benefits. They serve important and legitimate purposes for individuals and the American citizenry as a whole. However, these impulses work best in balance. That is also to say that both conservatives and liberals (at their radical extremes) are damaging. This country works best when all sides work to find a middle way – a balanced common ground that produces the greatest possible common good while still allowing the greatest possible individual liberty.

The terms *liberty* and *freedom* should not be misapplied. The privilege of personal choice cannot be separated from the obligation to public responsibility. Personal beliefs cannot be forced upon unwilling others. Internal thoughts and values are private. External acts are subject to limitations within a community. We defend personal liberties and freedoms up to the point that they tread on the personal liberties and freedoms of others. In this way, we create communities of common good and protect justice for all.

If this country's focus is entirely on conservative defense of traditions, the situation becomes too static and important changes become impossible. If this country's focus is entirely on the liberal defense of liberties, then the situation becomes too uncontrolled and important changes become impossible. If you will not plant your seed corn, you will eventually have to eat it and you will then have nothing.

Like the oriental yin/yang symbol, both conservatism and liberalism must coexist in balance. In fact, they contain and express each other. They complement each other, rather than compete. They are natural parts of the same dynamic system.

Here is an example of liberalism vs. conservation.

- In the spring, a farmer sows his field. This is an act of liberalism. He takes his resources and liberates them. To the extent that he takes the risk to liberally distribute his seed, it can grow. In the summer, the magic of earth's dynamic and bounteous systems causes the planted fields to increase and multiply. Abundance is created in growth as an unearned blessing of vitality and life.

- In the fall, the farmer harvests his field. This is an act of conservation. To the extent that he gathers in the crop and stores it in a safe place, it will be secure and safe. In the winter, the field is dormant. The farmer's resources are available to be rationed and consumed with caution.

Liberalism and conservation contain each other. In the spring, the farmer may reserve some seed to replant the field in case of some disaster or crop failure. This is conservation within liberalism. In the fall, the farmer may give up some of his crop to a needy neighbor or a common community storehouse. This is liberalism within conservation. And the circle is completed. And the circle is repeated. This is the general pattern of things.

However, in real life, there may be complications. There are always complications. Unexpected circumstances arise that require individuals and communities to improvise, change plans, and cooperate in new ways. Also, not everyone willingly chooses to cooperate in a balanced community. Some care about others. Some care only about themselves.

Our American system embraces (and must respond to) the needs, attitudes, and actions of millions of people. This produces a web of complex dynamics that cannot be explained or managed simply. Nonetheless, some generalizations allow us to cope with this constantly changing swirl of competing interests. So, without quibbling at every step about every exception, let me offer up one man's perspective on some real issues.

It is commendable that conservatives concern themselves with issues of individualism, family values, their faith and their communities. But, that is not the end of the conservative platform. Some men of wealth and power, seeking to continuously-increase their wealth and power have dressed themselves as wolves is sheep's clothing. There is no evident sufficiency to their grasping, covetous, greedy pursuit of ever-more wealth and power.

These rapacious wolves wrap their collective agenda in terms of personal freedom. They talk about individual liberties while they maneuver for their corporations to be legally treated as people. They talk about dismantling governmental meddling in citizens' lives while they lobby and bribe to dismantle governmental regulation of their predatory financial dealings, their discarding of industrial wastes, their looting of workers' pensions, their reduction of insurance benefits and their insider trading. It just keeps going on and on.

They tell you that they want to lower all taxes and then they lobby for loopholes, exemptions, special credits and subsidies for themselves. They argue that the government needs to favor "job creators" and then they send jobs to factories overseas. They make profit and financial gain sound like it will trickle down to every household. Instead, they hoard their profits, using them to buy other companies, dismantle them, consolidate their management and fire their workers.

I will say it again. It is commendable that conservatives profess to concern themselves with issues of individualism, family values, faith and group loyalty. However, that is not the end of our needs and concerns. We must also be involved in the entire range of people, changing circumstances and ideas that affect our lives and the interests of our children's children.

And, about individual liberties; be careful what you ask for; you may get more than you want. It's like what Oscar Wilde said, "When the gods wish to punish us, they answer our prayers." If you dismantle government, you will get fewer demands on your participation in society. You will need your guns to patrol your neighborhoods. You will have to personally threaten your wife's boss every time he decides to try to fondle her. You will have to repave your own streets and build your own bridges. You will have find your own books and teach your own children. You will have to lie in your own blood when you show up at a hospital after an automobile accident without insurance or cash.

There is a need and necessary place for government. Government is what defines how neighbors agree to serve each other. Government is the family making plans around the dinner table. It is the pie sale committee at your church. Government defines the responsibilities of increasingly large communities at city, county, state and federal levels. National governments participate in global problem solving when they make treaties with each other and create non-governmental organizations to help solve international problems.

Not every problem can be solved around the dinner table. In fact, you can count on the principle that problems can rarely be solved at the level at which they are created. This is another reason why multiple layers of government have been purposefully created and are functionally indispensable. Each increasing level of government is suited to serve additional societal needs.

We need other people. In fact, we need some kind of government for damn near everything that we cannot do by ourselves standing naked on the grass. When you meet someone else standing naked on the grass, you need to come to some agreement about what you will do next, and then again the next time you meet. Either that or you must resign yourself to always throw rocks at every stranger. On the other hand, if you are consistently aggressive, several strangers will get together and decide to take collective action to defend themselves for their own common good. They will agree on how to knock you down with rocks. Then they will tie you up and cast lots over who gets to eat your liver.

You see, common good is an even more wonderful thing than individual liberty. What some people in the radical right don't seem to understand is that individual liberties are protected by government. Our commitments to act for the common good are embodied in (and enforced by) government. Government is the most important and indispensable social concept ever invented after throwing rocks.

Throughout history, different balances of individual liberties and responsibility for common good have been tried. Some balances are more appropriate for small groups in good times and some are more appropriate for large groups in hard times. In a paradise, you can simply behave yourself and eat when you're hungry. In a war, you must be ready to give your life without hesitation at every moment.

So, the question is not one of extreme independence or obligation: "How can I get government off my back?" or "Which of my children shall I sacrifice to the gods?" The question is, "What balance of liberty and responsibility is best for the most people at this time and under these circumstances?"

Of course, the best balance is one that is always changing, and people will certainly have different opinions about the appropriate balance. Somebody is going to have to keep on top of that and keep making necessary adjustments. But then, that's why we need government. In fact, that's why we need multiple layers of government.

Some governments work from the top-down. An individual or group becomes rich enough and powerful enough to force their will upon the general population. In a benevolent autocracy, the ruler(s) serve as a father figure. Life is easy enough that everyone is content with his or her level of comfort and security – the trains run on time and life goes on.

More often though, the royals, priests, or other elites begin taking so much of the group's resources that life is not easy enough at all. The general population will eventually rise up. Whether there is a civil war or a revolution, the oppressors are killed or kicked out and, if some other strongman doesn't step in, the citizens take over and create a new government. This choice to create a government is, in fact, the history of our own Revolutionary War and Constitution.

A pure citizen government works from the bottom up. Abraham Lincoln described it as "of the people, by the people, and for the people." However, pure democracies tend to be impractical, even in small groups. Democracies usually express their idealism in some form of representative government. If there are adequate checks and balances, and the flexibility to adapt to changing circumstances over time, such representative democracies have usually worked well for industrialized nations.

This is a good place to point out that a representative democracy that emphasizes individual liberties is known as a "liberal democracy." During the American Revolution against King George of England, those maintaining loyalty to the royal elites were the "conservatives." This should give pause for thought but, let's move on for now.

What if wealthy and powerful elites eventually undermine the system of checks and balances? What if there is too much conservative resistance to change to allow problems to be corrected? Then, individual liberties are lost, the common good is neglected, extreme classes of wealth and poverty emerge, unfairness becomes endemic, and the citizens enter the path of protest, civil disobedience, civil war and revolution.

And the circle is completed. And the circle is repeated.

Before we go on, let's take one more swing at the necessity and purpose of robust and active governments. We don't have to look far. They are conveniently listed by our Founding Fathers – right up front in the Preamble of the *Constitution of the United States of America*. They are:

- Form a more perfect union
- Establish justice
- Insure domestic tranquility
- Provide for the common defense
- Promote the general welfare
- Secure the blessings of liberty to ourselves and our posterity

The implicit warning is that, if you seek to erode our governments' ability to perform these functions, you will, instead, promote disunion, injustice, domestic competition, weakened defenses, loss of common good, and the loss of liberties for individuals and future generations.

You would offer yourselves up in service to those who would take from the poor and give to the rich.

Our clear and present danger does not lie in government itself. The danger lies in those who would twist government to their own craven advantage. Our goal should not be to dismantle government, but to strengthen its ability to address the needs of the general population for the common good. Our government was designed to be the solution, not the problem. Our rule of law is an indispensable safeguard for the defense of liberties. We need to work hard to make government work well.

In America today, we are facing an assault by some elites to accumulate controlling wealth and power. Allowed to go unopposed and uncorrected, this widening difference of wealth and power may become intolerably extreme. Common citizens may feel so oppressed and unfairly treated that they rise up in a new revolution.

In fact, it is these very issues of unfairness that the conservative elites are creating and that most citizens (both conservative and liberal) are feeling. Ironically, instead of uniting to oppose those elites who are acting exclusively in their own selfish interests, the two parties divide against each other and against themselves. This is tragic.

Happily, not all people of wealth and power feel motivated to keep on acquiring for the sheer gratification of ever more wealth and power. Some have decided to act from a liberal disposition. I am deeply moved by the list of seventy uncommonly wealthy families who have signed "The Giving Pledge" to give the majority of their wealth to philanthropy. You can see this for yourself at GivingPledge.org.

We should thank liberals such as these for fighting in defense of individual liberties: emancipation of slaves, workers' rights (including the 40-hour week and child-labor laws), voting rights, civil rights, amendments to the constitution guaranteeing additional freedoms, and much more.

We also have liberals to thank for defending the common good: independence of the 13 Colonies from England, public schools and universities, rural electrification, national parks and forests, the Interstate Highway System, the Marshall Plan, Social Security, bank deposit insurance, dams, canals, and other infrastructure, emergency loans after disasters, public first responders, and much more.

Many people eat up the pack of lies they are being fed about liberals. Stop a moment and think about who has been serving up this slander. Think about what their motives might be. Think about how outraged you should be.

If you are already a liberal, get a firm grip on your meek, mild, compromising ass and saddle up. Superman didn't use his abilities to get rich and powerful. Like a liberal, he chose to take a stand and fight for truth, justice and the American way. He was a true liberal radical, and he never apologized for it.

If you do your research into the roots of liberal philosophy, you find the love and defense of personal liberties. You find a strong defense for "a private sphere representing the limits to public action." This does not become imbalanced so that individuals are guaranteed the right to do anything they want to anyone they want. Instead, liberalism seeks to stay balanced so that all are protected from abuse.

Balanced liberalism defends the individual while asking us to also assume responsibility for each other. This is the glory of community and neighborliness. This is the shining light of Good Samaritans, uniting to care about each individual – and agreeing to contribute a fair share for that purpose. Balanced liberalism seeks to protect you from exploitation. But, balanced liberalism also intends to stand in your way, like the incorruptible sheriff in a frontier town, if *you* exploit or abuse others.

Liberals are smeared and vilified with words such as "Radical," "Communist," and "Socialist." This is unfair. There are very few people in the United States who actually want the state to own the means of production. We believe that enterprising people should be encouraged to build, create, grow, and earn profits and be allowed to retain a share of their profits.

On the other hand, businesses benefit from resources in the public commons such as water and electrical utilities, fire and police protection, roads and bridges, libraries, public buildings and national security forces. Businesses, as well as individuals, should be taxed fairly to cover a reasonable (and responsible) share of the public resources from which they benefit.

Who does not believe that people and businesses should behave responsibly toward others around them? Who does not understand that governmental regulations must be created and enforced to the degree that you and your neighbors are put at risk? There should be a good guy with a badge in every town. And, if he organizes a posse, we should be willing to ride out with him and have his back.

So, please, inform yourselves about issues and candidates. Register if you haven't – and vote. I have to tell you that, at present, I don't have confidence in the good faith or good will of the radical right. I have to ask this: whether you vote for liberals or vote for moderates, please vote for men and women of conscience and integrity, who care about the welfare of others and who offer themselves in true service to their communities.

Vote for optimists who believe in the potential of this nation to work hard, succeed and prosper. Vote for public servants who deeply *get it* that we are all in this together and must care about the welfare of others.

Vote for virtuous people who embrace carefully considered values. Values of family. Spiritual values. Values of community – but more than that – people whose compassion embraces entire regions, their entire nation and the welfare of all their brothers and sisters on this fragile earth. Make "Peace on earth. Goodwill toward men" a heartfelt goal, not an empty platitude.

In this time of increasing global dependency and crisis, we must open ourselves to all humanity, to all life on our fragile planet. For, if we do not choose to all live together, we shall, assuredly, all perish together.

Why Everybody (except angry white males) Should Vote Democratic

This was written in the spring of 2012 - The names have changed, but the sentiments are worth running up the flag pole again.

The Democratic Party represents the best long-term interests of the majority of U.S. citizens. Even if you don't like liberal attitudes, diversity or permissiveness, a Republican vote, this year, is against your best interests. Most angry white males are in their own tightly self-constructed world. You can love them and feed them, but I don't think you can do much to change their minds just now, so never mind.

I don't begrudge "Tea Party" sympathizers their frustrated state of mind. Times are hard and they have been getting harder for the last several decades – along with the pace of change. Everybody is struggling and unhappy. But, this is not a good time to seriously think that we can go back to family farms and small-shop manufacturing.

Neither is it helpful to start arming yourself because your President is black, some of your neighbors speak Spanish or Vietnamese or some Muslims are building a place of worship. Really, just what are you planning to do with all of that firepower?

My wife rescued a small dog last year. We knew that the dog would eventually quit trying to jump on the cats and the cats would quit hissing at her – but, the critters only knew that they were anxious and confused right now. One kitty wouldn't come out of the laundry room for several days. They will never be great friends, but they can now nap all together without making a fuss. My point is that we humans ought to be able to do even better.

The bottom line is that there is no going back. Regressive policies put us into many of our current problems and, if brought back, will only make things worse. These bad policies include tax cuts for the very rich, allowing businesses to buy political influence, unjustified (and unfunded) wars, and trashing regulatory protections against pollution, exploitation of others, and financial risk-taking. The Republican Party used to have conservative and liberal wings, but they currently seem hell-bent on charging in the wrong direction. By "bad" and "wrong" I mean against the long-term best interests of the majority of American citizens.

In the past, progressive activism won for us the best of what enabled individuals, small businesses, and minority groups to seize the American Dream. Progressive policies brought us budget surpluses under President Clinton. Progressive policies turned-around the recent economic death-spiral. We may whine that the recovery is too slow, but we should be consciously grateful to still be moving forward.

Mitt Romney, despite being a faithful family- and church-man, has not demonstrated that he has the best interests of most citizens at heart. In fact, his flaunted business experience is in reaping profits for his investors. Romney pioneered techniques for outsourcing jobs, evading taxes, plundering assets and promoting himself. He is willing to feed the worst greed of the rich elite, and the tacit bigotry of the far right wing. Romney remains the choice of greedy rich men and angry white men.

Naturally, President Obama can't go around bragging, "The economy would have been worse." But really, it would have been much, much worse. It is a pity that we haven't seen, in our TV shows and newspapers, the litany of ways that the "Obama stimulus" has made a difference in every community. Win-win projects were chosen that both kept people working and advanced our country's long-term needs. Vital research was funded. Our electrical grid got updates. Wind and solar generation projects got tax breaks. But, too often, when we got a new bridge, when the school was repaired, when two police officers were not laid off, nobody noticed that the stimulus made it happen.

The president is not endowed with an endless supply of magic fairy dust – just the headship of the Executive Branch. The fact of the matter is that we have been well served. President Obama wisely selected experienced people for his transition team and government. He was willing to recruit and listen to Republicans. He was even determined to convince Hillary Clinton, his opponent in the primaries, to serve with him.

Presidents can exercise limited policy discretion, but it is our Senators and Congressmen who make the laws. Or, not so much recently. In fact, House and Senate Republicans have invested a great deal of effort in obstructing American recovery efforts – even voting against their own earlier best ideas and present best interests. We should stop voting for those Republican obstructionists who would inflict damage on their country for the sole purpose of getting a black man out of "their" Whitehouse. President Obama's biggest mistake was believing, at first, that Republican "public servants" in Congress would eventually come around and work with him to actually serve the public.

We can't seriously believe that President Obama hates this country, or plans to spend us down the drain, or sell us to China. We *can* believe that our economic pump needed priming and that he did the job without a lot of waste. In fact, many economists believe that the stimulus should have been bigger. Insiders report that during the design of the stimulus, President Obama's guidance was to get the fastest, best and most future-building bang for the buck. He consistently warned department heads to not use it to justify increases in their budgets.

We can't let the big banking dogs eat all the dog food. We can't let the big-business foxes run the hen house. We can't let austerity eat our seed corn. We can't continue to let financiers gamble with our money, keeping the profits and sticking the rest of us with their losses. We can't let well-organized zealots force their religious doctrines into our private lives. Vote Democratic this year.

We may have suffered whiplash when President Obama suddenly left behind the hopey-changey rhetoric of the campaign and dived whole-souled into the wonky-techy work of getting domestic and foreign policy right. But, we didn't suffer from his commitment to looking out for the long-term best interests of our country. Vote Democratic this year.

Reason for Optimism

I feel strongly about unresolved issues (such as climate change) and write about them with a sense of urgency. Still, I hold a personal optimism that problems will eventually be addressed and adequately resolved. Let me tell you a story.

Back in the early 1990s, I belonged to an engineering department of Amoco Oil Company and started agitating about what eventually became known as the "Y2K problem." That is, most computerized data tables and program algorithms held dates using only the last two digits of the year. The problem was that dates after 1999 would appear to be a hundred years earlier than they actually were. The vast majority of computer programs would malfunction if they were not rewritten. No bank, florist or traffic light could be assumed to be immune.

My hair was on fire about this issue but I didn't seem to be getting any traction with my management. But, about 18 months before crisis time, the whole world seemed to spontaneously generate a burst of awareness and activity. Specialty consulting and contracting firms suddenly appeared, along with emergency appropriations from senior management, to undertake the work. Some program applications were systematically combed and rewritten; some were simply replaced with newer programs. It was an inconceivably massive and complex international effort.

A few companies suffered temporarily for their inattention or incompetence, but most of the world got the job done. January 1, 2000 came and went. Most of our lights didn't go out and our bank deposits didn't disappear. There was a related story about an airplane on cruise control that turned itself upside down when it crossed the equator. The world gave a collective sigh of relief, shook their heads at all the silliness and tucked in to watch reruns of *Bonanza* and comment that nothing much had come of all the fuss over *New Coke* either.

In the local news today, there is a new project to build 170 wind turbines on the slightly higher ground just north of my small Iowa town. Local governments in Southern California have committed to make the greater Los Angeles basin energy- and water-independent by 2050. It's almost enough to make me an optimist.

Computers: Servants or Masters?

Computers help us to be (or appear to be) smarter. Of course, they (1) help us to count and calculate faster. They also (2) expand our capacity to remember. Even when they seem to make us lazy about having to memorize facts, there is no denying they give us rapid access to what we, and the rest of humanity, have recorded. Further, digital technology helps us to rapidly (3) find, connect to and communicate with distant people. The equivalent of Dick Tracy's wrist communicator is now widely available. My goodness.

All three of the above are examples of "external human augmentation." My former career was heavily involved with all manner of computers, from micro-controllers in instruments to IBM mainframes. Now, in an era of "big data," computers are combing through unimaginably large pools of information to predict business opportunities, invent undiscovered chemical reactions and recognize patterns of weather, disease, and crime. Computers predict the kinds of advertisements that will make us pause and look. They can build custom products to our specifications and translate any web page into dozens of languages.

In 1986, I discovered the article, "Computing as a Tool for Human Augmentation" by W. J. Doherty and W. G. Pope in the *IBM Systems Journal*. They pointed out that, "The IBM Thomas J. Watson Research Center in Yorktown, New York, has experienced a factor of twenty times increase in the past ten years in the amount of time its people spend using computers interactively in their work. This is twice the penetration rate of television in the 1950s. A similar degree of penetration is expected to happen in the rest of industry in the next ten years." Boy, were they right.

We've clearly gotten used to computers augmenting our capacities. In some ways, technology has given us super-human abilities. Smart-phone apps can predict that you are about to be hungry, remember your favorite kinds of food, search in an unfamiliar neighborhood, and recommend a restaurant you will like… or find restaurants that people like those in your social networks have recommended.

Most of us have gotten quite dependent on our computer applications, as well. People habitually use GPS devices to find their way while driving. Now, people are even beginning to attach computer displays to their eyeglasses and researchers are working to put displays into contact lenses.

Pieces of large self-guided farm equipment already use GPS to drive in straight lines across fields. Automobile manufacturers are almost ready to make car-to-car communication and automation a standard feature. Inevitably, we will be riding in self-driving transport robots.

Several states and countries are creating standards, writing regulations and running experimental trials for self-driving vehicles. It's already obvious they will be safer. We can expect to rent rides in vehicles with no steering wheels that show up when you want them. Their costs will be amortized across a large number of users rather than a single owner. When not needed, they can wander off to slurp up an electrical recharge or park themselves out of the way.

As with every technology, there will be issues of roll-out, shake-out, resistance, adaptation and acceptance. These are well-known and well-understood issues of change management. Change happens.

Researchers are now investigating the best ways to mix robot and human workers. The robots don't seem to care too much, but humans prefer that the robots seem to be polite and do most of the repetitive and uncomfortable tasks. In fact, humans even seem to prefer that automated systems tell them what to do next when a computer's efficiency algorithms exceed a human worker's planning capacity.

People are also demonstrating they prefer a sufficiently talented robotic companion to being alone. They will sometimes confess their anxieties and health conditions more readily to an automated analyst- or nurse-proxy. They will sometimes trust the judgment of a diagnostic system that has permanent access to libraries of medical data over a haphazard consultation with a harried and hurried live doctor.

I don't expect that, in the end, either robots or humans will fall solidly into the categories of servants or masters. Computers and robots will be our collaborators. They will be used increasingly in tasks that are too hazardous, annoying or complicated for most people. It will be a strange dance and a wild ride but, typically, most of us eventually accept and embrace new convenience technology.

Is Big Data Dangerous?

I have been giving away personal data all my life. In 1959, when I first filled out a coupon in the back of a comic book, I started getting related offers in the mail. It is no surprise that computers make keeping these lists easier and that social networks collect the life details we share. "Big data" computer algorithms now connect the mass of breadcrumbs we leave behind, making assumptions about our habits and preferences.

For many years, marketers and advertisers have been collecting and using information about us and we have been cheerfully cooperating. Subscribe to *Bride* magazine and wedding service companies will know your intentions before your boyfriend does. Today, free apps on our cell phones offer us remarkable services and we eagerly install and use them. However, do not be surprised that, "If the app is free, *you* are the product."

Privacy, like virginity, may be highly esteemed and valiantly protected, but it is easily surrendered in a cascade of momentary indiscretions and, in so doing, irretrievably lost. Modesty and decency dictate that our rush to do something useful with our current collective gush of personal disclosure will eventually find moderation and dignity. Until then, many people will feel over-exposed. You can imagine them sitting in corners, clasping great cloaks around themselves – eyes darting suspiciously at passing strangers.

Ironically, while we may demand our own privacy, we expect openness and transparency from governments, businesses and each other. We want to have public access to all government data, disclosure of corporate balance sheets and information about sex offenders in our neighborhoods.

The theory is that openness gives light that protects us from dark places where hidden evil breeds corruption. Political candidates were once named in smoke-filled back rooms, businesses conspired for unethical advantage, and families sequestered themselves in suburban fortresses without learning their neighbors' names. In the last few weeks, people have begun campaigning to have police officers wear cameras to record their interactions with citizens as a defense against abuse of authority.

A new generation no longer assumes that they require private homes with hoards of private stuff. They are learning to re-engage with others in communities of sharing and collaboration. Young adults often prefer to share housing, transportation and ideas. They are discovering the camaraderie, productivity and satisfaction of working together in voluntary groups. And, they are more-willing to disclose themselves socially.

The payoff for embracing "big data" is beginning to emerge as it rapidly matures. Initially, large data sets of personal information were only imagined to be of use for business marketing or government surveillance. Now, new kinds of databases and query languages are able to digest unimaginable quantities of event records and find important and useful patterns where any human would only see random noise.

As examples, Twitter trends reveal outbreaks of infectious diseases several days faster than doctors can update reports to a central database. Big data is being used to optimize urban planning, medical diagnosis, social services, preventive maintenance, air quality, traffic control, crime reduction and automated language translation.

As sensors and computers become ubiquitous and the "Internet of everything" takes root, our systems are beginning to anticipate our needs. Google Now can analyze your usual commute home and suggest alternate routes that avoid local traffic congestion. Refrigerators know their contents and suggest buying more milk on the way home or discarding leftovers that are too old. Amazon has filed for a patent on a system that could take the initiative to ship something that they think you will want to order.

Big Data does not need to be considered a great Orwellian assault on privacy and free will. Instead, it offers the capacity to extend the age-old tools of everyday marketing to the nuts and bolts of making our lives easier and more productive.

A Criticism of Literary Criticism

While in college, I took an obligatory literature class. I'm sure the school believed that this would make me a better person. Well, actually, it probably did. I read some good stuff and then some other stuff and then I had to think about it. So far, so good.

However, you can't escape a literature class without being exposed to the insanity of 'literary criticism.' At first, I tried to take it seriously. I tried to imitate my mentors and masters. But, the more I tried, the more I cried. No, no, no. This was not an occupation for reasonable people with something useful to occupy their time.

I threw a hissy-fit. I wrote and submitted the following:

> While preparing for this class, I reviewed parts of the textbook *Contemporary Literary Criticism: Literary and Cultural Studies*, by Robert Con Davis and Ronald Schleifer. It seemed intimidating – obtuse – maybe recursive. Take for instance, part of paragraph two from page eleven of "Introduction: a Study of Criticism at the Present Time," which asserts: "The scandal presented by contemporary criticism, which goes to the heart of the ontological difficulty, can be described as a radical division, a split-the "devastating experience," Miller describes, "of a transformation of the scene which leaves it nevertheless exactly the same." The pervasive figure of the split indicates a sense in contemporary theory of a fundamental division within texts, specifically as regards their involvement in time (Davis and Schleifer 11)." Or, consider part of paragraph three on page nine: "it is a commonplace of contemporary thought that so much contemporary criticism and cultural critique – de Man's literary studies, Kristeva's semiotics, Derrida's "deconstructive" philosophy, the psychoanalysis of Lacan, Jameson's Marxist analysis, Cixous's feminist discourse – should be difficult to follow. (Davis and Schleifer 9)."

Yeah, tell me about difficult to follow. Overcome with trepidation and defensive aggression, I jotted down the following observations:

- Literary criticism is as bereft of meaning and consequence as playing cards, and especially analyzing the sequence of hands following their play.
- The textbook specifically recommends focusing on some single quality or aspect of an artistic work. This reminds me strongly of blind men describing an elephant, each from the perspective of the body part with which they are in touch.
- The reader can never actually know the process the writer went through in producing the finished product. He can only guess or peer at it from a distance – through a jaundiced eye and a single, very personal, perspective.
- A literary critic can say anything that comes to mind or propose any connection that a clever fellow can invent. There is very little anyone else can do to contradict or disabuse him of his position.
- A literary critic is someone who takes an image of a work, reprints it, cuts it into 1,000 jigsaw puzzle pieces, throws out the greater part of them, and prides himself in explaining it, reproducing it, and making sense of the original work, with only a handful of the original pieces consciously at hand for reference.
- Literary criticism is worse than plagiarism. With plagiarism, one takes a work that they admire and allows it to be perceived as their own. A literary critic takes an admirable work and robs it of its coherence. Dissected, he displays its parts, presuming to be a self-appointed master – fit to interpret and judge the original writer, or worse, preempting another reader's impression and interpretation.
- Literary criticism is like painting an old hand-hewn and craftsmen-worked furniture piece that has lost its luster. It's no improvement to the original; it only defaces it and distracts from its original beauty.

- Literary criticism seems to be an artless and self-centered indulgence. Lacking creativity, it depends on someone else's work. Lacking substance, it occurs solely in the critic's mind. Lacking grace and charm it rarely consents to speak well of the object of its attention. Lacking enduring satisfaction, the critic moves on, looking for yet another victim for his callous dissection.

Having disgorged that bile, I reminded myself that I dislike people who, in hubris, are overly proud of their ignorance.

Every field has its practitioners – justly proud of their ability to make intricate distinctions within their field of expertise. This is commendable and not to be despised. If you cannot reduce and analyze a thing in some detail, how can you know when you have found a different (or better) one? You show me your list of archaic irregular verbs and I will show you my collection of pastel colored cat teapots (really).

Looking back to the Preface, I am comforted by paragraph two on page ix, "Students who do well with this material not only recognize criticism as an activity to be performed but also see it as important. Other students tend to regard criticism as simply a body of knowledge to be learned, in which failure is always lurking so that each new critical position for scholastic effort could be something to confuse and confound them (Roberts and Jacobs ix)." Damn straight.

I'm beginning to understand that criticism may properly be considered a kind of stylized conversation. My public speaking class teacher used to say that public speaking is like a conversation between a speaker and a listener. She talked a great deal about the types of feedback that the speaker receives. My literature teacher also maintained that literature was a conversation between the writer and the reader.

It occurs to me that the Japanese have a long tradition of using stylized conversations. What is said and how it is said can have a precise form. This is true for more than just the Japanese tea ceremony or certain social interactions. When I lived in South Texas, I noticed some stylized conversations and greetings. For instance, "How are you doing?" is always followed by, "Just fine. Thank you." This is so rote that, from cynical experience, I can testify that one could say "Good morning." and still get the response "Just fine. Thank you."

A few years have passed and my attitude toward literary criticism has not much improved. For starters, my college textbook classified literature into four genres. (Roberts and Jacobs 2) At the same time, my wife's third graders were being given a list of eight genres. Which, now, is a more finely-graduated curriculum? Why shouldn't literary criticism be considered a genre in its own right? My god, I've invented number nine.

I'm tempted to stick to my Agatha Christie mysteries, Batman comics and George R. R. Martin romps. George is the guy who wrote, "A reader lives a thousand lives before he dies… The man who never reads lives only one." Yeah. Now that's the thing. You shouldn't read for the perverse intent of desecrating some story with a dental pick. *You should read for the vicarious voyeuristic gestalt of losing yourself in another's skin.* Somebody should make a note of that. Someday, it will be in books of quotations.

And, a "conversation between the writer and the reader?" Posh. If I am to be obliged to have a conversation with Falkner, Kerouac or Giesel, they are welcome to rise up and meet me half way. Otherwise, I'll read them or I won't. (Well, okay, maybe an exception for Giesel for he must surely abide among the gods.)

Oh, by the way. I'm a living author. You can find me. You can hire me to come give talks. You can write to me. I'll think about what you say and you'll inspire me to write some more. Now *that's* having a conversation!

If It Ain't Broke, Don't Fix It

I ran errands today. Every step helped to clarify a distinction between conservative and liberal values that has been itching in the corners of my mind: *Conservatives like to harvest what they can; they tend to avoid risk and evade personal responsibility for needed change. Liberals like to create and build; they tend to take personal and collective initiative when change is needed.*

I live in a conservative rural area and do business in a nearby conservative town. Everywhere I stopped to take care of an errand, I met a situation that needed improvement and people who felt no responsibility for making things better.

My wife, Dianna, and I had decided to cancel our regional newspaper subscription. The circulation representative told her that it was easier if we just let funds, already in our account, run out and so we agreed to accept daily delivery of birdcage liner for another six weeks. Naturally, we were surprised to receive a renewal notice in the mail. I took the invoice into the circulation department. A slightly huffy lady told me not to worry, that I had a stop-date card in the drawer and that's just the way their computer works. I was irritated but held my tongue. I'm a retired computer systems manager and have strong sensibilities about responsible data management.

My second stop was to drop off ten shirts to be laundered on hangers with starch. My receipt was almost illegible; the thermal print head had probably been going bad for several years. I pointed out that the ticket indicated "boxed, no starch." A clearly indifferent young woman told me not to worry, that she makes notes on the tickets, that's what they go by and that's just the way their computer works. I rolled my eyes and started feeling more than a little disenchanted.

My third stop was to pick up piano method books for one of Dianna's music students. A regional music company keeps a branch store in town and we generally like to patronize local businesses. They didn't have everything on my list but agreed to do a computer search of inventory at the main store. As the process dragged on, the clerk looked sheepish and said, "The database is *usually* kind of slow."

As we waited, I copped a glance at the connectors on the back of the computer; it was pretty old. The printer used a Centronics parallel cable. You can go into a computer store these days and the typical kid at the counter has never heard of "Centronics." I asked the clerk what operating system was on his machine. It was Windows 95.

We looked into each other's eyes with the comprehension and compassion of beleaguered and impotent men. I offered, "I guess your computer department doesn't love you." He lowered his eyes in shame. It was a truth that would have been better left unspoken. We eventually gave up waiting for his computer to finish the search. That evening, I got a better price and faster shipping from Amazon.

Stop number four was to pay my monthly rental for a piece of medical equipment. I could have mailed-in a check but I prefer to do on-line transfers, which this company's systems don't support. Besides, they were on my route; I would deliver their money in person. The invoice I held was printed on tractor-fed, fan-fold, three-copy, carbonless self-duplicating paper. They stamped the back copy with a "Paid" stamp and returned it to me. I could read the stamp, but the print was illegible. By now, I was filled with the glorious fire of righteous intolerance. I asked to see whomever made decisions about computer technology. It seems I needed to talk to Michael.

"Michael, thank you for seeing me. I'm a customer here and rent a C-PAP machine. I'm also a writer and preparing an essay on business technology. Has anybody ever suggested updates such as using a laser printer to produce legible invoices?"

"Well yes, that has come up several times and several companies have tried to sell us new systems. But, what we have has been working for us since 1980 and, you know, 'If it's not broke, don't fix it.'" This was an obvious false premise. It might still be in harness but, of course, it was broken.

My realization blossomed into the radiance and certainty of a full epiphany. I was swimming in the evident demonstration of one of conservatism's cardinal characteristic concepts – the faulty foundation of fundamentalism's flawed fallacies. Conservatives prefer to collect and consume instead of creating or constructing. They will even, with unsullied conscience, harvest resources held in common and generated by the labor or loss of others. They prefer to exhaust a resource until, finally, they are forced by desperate circumstance to improvise in an emergency. It goes against their grain to anticipate future or collective problems and take personal initiative or work as part of a community to prepare for needed change.

Another realization erupted to compound and confirm my fresh insight. I used to work as an instrumentation and control system craftsman at a gasoline refinery. The place was rusting in place and, quite literally, falling apart. We were often denied budget money to replace or repair aging equipment. Management usually preferred to pay extra to use an emergency appropriation when pieces of equipment inevitably failed.

For instance, we couldn't get money to repair a gas flare ignition system. Instead, a member of the fire crew would be sent up the hill to dip an arrow into a bucket of oil, light it, and shoot it over the top of the flare tower. Employees and neighbors started saying the company should just shut the place down.

As it turned out, senior management was planning exactly that. One manager eventually stopped my persistent pleas for maintenance funding by admitting that we were running under a policy of "deferred maintenance." Oh, I realized, they weren't all crazy-stupid; they were co-conspirators in a deliberate and dangerous plan to harvest the remaining capacity of the equipment until it (and possibly some expendable personnel) died.

The company built a special machine to add contaminated dirt to coke and asphalt products while staying just within maximum permissible "ash" content. They bought and demolished homes surrounding the refinery as people found gasoline seeping into their basements. They eventually closed the place altogether, wrote-off decommissioning expenses against taxes, and actually made money by drilling shallow wells and recovering old spilled oil.

Considering these as typical examples, the policies and platforms of the current Republican Party begin to make sense. For instance, they prefer to avoid investing in infrastructure – "kicking the can down the road" instead. This feels very much like my refinery's policy of "deferred maintenance." This feels very much like the operating tactics of private equity "vampire capitalists." Will businessmen actually be allowed to run this country into the ground, extracting all possible capital, before moving on to new profit opportunities?

You stop investing in something when you decide you don't need it. You start to choose hospice and palliative care when Grandma no longer has sufficient value. You stop planting trees on a mountain when you plan to scrape off its top for mining.

Conservatives often covet the profits from privatizing public services. Instead of trying to make government work better, conservatives try to obstruct our government to make it look worse. It is easier, in the short run, to harvest and consume existing resources than to invest in rebuilding systems to be useful or sustainable into our children's futures. This is exploitation, not conservation as you might expect from the core concept of the word "conservative."

Would you trust your future to people whose values still include, "I saw it first – finder's keepers;" "It's not my responsibility;" "If it ain't broke, don't fix it;" "Well, you're not using it;" "Take what you can now and screw the future?"

In Praise of the Public Sector

I'm in a particularly grumpy mood this morning as I think about the almost-completed water tower maintenance in our small town and the inconvenience that came with it. Today's newspaper had several critical letters to the editor.

I have a more-appreciative attitude. I am grateful for the wisdom and courage of our Mayor and City Council to undertake this (very necessary) project. They knew up-front it would bring out the worst in armchair critics and whiners. The fact of the matter is that the temporary inconveniences were an entirely unavoidable part of completing the job. It's what we needed to do. We ought to be thanking our public servants instead of giving them grief.

Sometimes we forget that government, the widely despised "public sector," is really us – you and me and those of our neighbors who (for some deficit of sanity) feel compelled to render an extra measure of service to our communities. What thanks do our public servants get? A general unwillingness to grant them the resources and cooperation they need to fully achieve the many responsibilities we demand of them.

It is the private sector that rakes their leaves into the street, lets their dogs bark and their cats breed. It is the private sector that drives on roads, disturbs the peace, consumes clean water, flushes their toilets and makes babies. Yet, it is the public sector that gets called on for animal control, cleaning leaves out of storm drains and providing utilities. The private sector teaches our children to read and do fractions while also building their social skills and nurturing their love of learning.

And then, the private sector often turns around and protests that tax revenues are a plot by "them" to rob "us" of hard-earned wages. And then, they compound the insult: For many whiners, these "hard earned wages" are actually tax-free government-provided benefits such as social security, Medicare, or food assistance.

Harrumph. If we keep undermining our public sector, we could succeed in earning the privilege of always hauling and boiling our own water, teaching our children calculus and paving our own streets while guarding our own doors. Oh, and are we actually ready to grow our own gardens or starve? Are we ready to face the cold alternatives of staying healthy or dying quickly?

On the national level, how is it that our economy has been declining for thirty years now and yet a single man, in office for only a few years, is "failed" for not waving a magic wand and suddenly making everything somehow completely better? How is it that #43, who fought two wars and funded massive and repeated tax cuts on our credit card, who cut banking regulations and presided over the resulting financial collapse, gets the benefit of a helpless shoulder shrug and a Teflon coated record?

The thing that gives me a measure of courage is the hope that progressive policies may yet have a snowball's chance in hell of moving us forward. I'm in the mood for comfort for the afflicted. Keep your chin up. There is always hope... especially if we are each willing to support the inconvenience and effort that is necessary to get us, all together, where we need to go.

Forgetting the Future

I recently wrote about the important effect that our emotional approach to "now" has on our happiness. Guilt about our past should inform our choices, but not overwhelm our ability to enjoy a better life. "Now" is precious because it is our only opportunity to enjoy the moment, do something virtuous or make a decision to improve the future.

There are those in the new-age movement who seem obsessed with the current moment that is *now*. These people hold that, because the past and future cannot be directly experienced, they are no better than illusions — the only thing that can happen is happening now. This is true enough, as far as it goes. What we experience, how we interpret it and what we do about it, are the only dynamic parts of life. How blessed it is to be always aware of opportunities to "smell the roses" — a little narcissistic, but nice.

I believe that the whole point of remembering the past and experiencing the present is to learn, act in the image of God's love, do good, and create a better future for ourselves and others. That is, a well-lived life is the act of persistently creating something better. Ken Wilber, a contemporary philosopher, recently pointed out that, "The way you approach the present isn't just determined by the way you approach the past, but by the way you approach the future. The richer conception of the future you have, the richer your life in the present becomes."

Do you have a clear vision of where you're going in life? Consider Alice's conversation with the Cheshire Cat from *Alice in Wonderland*:

> "Would you tell me, please, which way I ought to go from here?"

> "That depends on where you want to get to," said the Cat.

> "I don't much care where," said Alice.

> "Then it doesn't matter which way you go," said the Cat.

This wisdom should seem so obvious that we would all regularly reflect, with sincere purpose, on where we want to go and how we are planning to get there. However, we often see a very different attitude. There are those who simply want to go through life with the bare minimum of hassle, responsibility or obligation. As a teacher, my wife referred to this attitude of indifference as "unengaged." The unengaged student only wanted to do the least amount of work required to get by.

Sometimes, you can't avoid facing a choice and having to make an unexpected decision. Yogi Berra recommended that, "If you come to a fork in the road, take it." But, there is no purpose to walking around blindly. As the first-century Roman philosopher, Seneca is quoted, "Luck is where the crossroads of opportunity and preparation meet." Said another way, if a door opens to you, will you be prepared to recognize it and walk through?

We should ask what kind of future we imagine for ourselves; our families; our community; our world? Does it promote happy, healthy and productive lives? Are we behaving as if we recognize and appreciate our gifts? Are we caring for the garden that is the world in which we live? Do we have established goals for a better future? Do our decisions persistently move us in that direction?

The Future of Unsustainable Development

Most of us have heard the phrase "sustainable development" and perhaps a little about initiatives related to sustainable development such as Agenda 21 and the Earth Charter. Many communities are exploring these principles in the hope of heading off (or at least moderating) future catastrophes.

Critics of organized sustainable development describe it as a massive international conspiracy to deprive us of individual and capitalistic rights. Actually, ignoring sustainability could actually deprive us of freedoms. In fact, if we don't start making better decisions and addressing important sustainability problems now, we certainly *will* lose many options that we currently take for granted. Either someone will step in to save us from ourselves, or abandon us to the consequences that we bring down upon our own heads. My bet is that several billion people will die in crisis and conflict before we adapt to the effects of our changing climate.

Since we started living in communities, part of the deal has always been that we can't always do or take just anything we want. In America, our constitution grants generous freedoms and liberties, but civility and justice demand that our rights end in the vicinity of where our neighbors' rights begin. The authority the American founding fathers wisely gave us to regulate ourselves through government ensures important protections to us all.

Some insist that all natural resources are given by God to man to own, subdue, and have dominion over (Genesis 1:28). Further, they argue that man was given the physical and mental powers to accomplish this dominion. However, this same scripture instructed him to be fruitful, multiply and fill the earth – with no mention of limits. This sounds to me like a command to exercise responsible, sustainable stewardship rather than a grant of free license to dig, build, spew, kill and destroy.

Frankly, America has thrived economically for centuries based on the exploitation of its abundant land, rivers, trees and mineral resources.

However, Native Americans discovered how little that freedoms and rights mattered when private and business interests decided that, "they weren't using it, so why not just take it?" Now that national and global resources are becoming scarce, who will be next to suffer from the greed of exploiters, and who will we depend on to stop them?

Do we personally exploit? Automobiles, the open road and cheap gasoline have been taken for granted as definingly American. A gas-guzzling vehicle is a public symbol of status and achievement. Free public roads are also taken for granted. We act as if we deserve the unlimited option to live, work, play, shop, commute, and just drive around at will.

However, continued, unrestrained and unregulated exploitation and consumption are not sustainable. We may think that only people we don't know and don't care about are going to suffer. The fact is that the vast majority of Americans are already experiencing the effects of unsustainability. Our children will certainly suffer profoundly.

Only the very rich have the resources to consume, waste and pollute conspicuously without immediate personal consequence. Believe me, they are fighting for every political edge to protect their place of preeminent advantage and control.

Do you care about your grandchildren? Start explaining to them now about the importance of sustainability. And, introduce them to the principles behind Agenda 21 and the Earth Charter.

Will Real Wars Come Back?

Have you noticed that our thinking about war has gotten softer? These days, our wars tend to earn euphemisms such as: border skirmish, police action, regime change, nation building, civil uprising, popular revolution and gorilla opposition. Similarly, killing becomes targeting, eliminating, taking out, and collateral damage. Obviously, the idea of war is becoming too repulsive to be named for what it is without shame. Anymore, you don't often see Group A attacking Group B with the intent of killing or enslaving everyone in their path and taking all of their land and property. Yeah, "real war" used to really mean something.

It used to be that horsemen pounded off the barren steppes to pillage great swathes of quiet villages. European colonizers often summarily claimed whatever they "discovered," demanding its resources for themselves, and usually were more than rude to its current inhabitants. We try to not remember how recently indigenous peoples of the American continents were slaughtered or driven from their lands and how recently slavery drove agricultural economies.

The incomprehensible violence of World War II so scared everybody that we all just *had* to find ways to not do *that* again. Now, several generations later, we are still feeling good about returning pieces of art to the grandchildren of people who had their homes plundered. Parliaments and presidents are still feeling obliged to make apologies for atrocities committed by their predecessors in other times.

Real war is all about violent conquest, and it produces victors and the vanquished. And yes, this is a very bad state of affairs. However, isn't there some point at which the victors stop oppressing their victims and the vanquished stop seeking revenge? A real war happened. Somebody won. We have to eventually move on and work together to make life better for all those disenfranchised survivors and restrain those whose greed or hate would create injustice and misery to others.

What will we do as sea levels rise, deserts take over cropland and essential services fail? Refugees will want to immigrate to more-hospitable areas as a matter of survival. What will happen to Phoenix when the American Southwest starts to resemble Death Valley? What will happen when Iowa becomes a dust bowl and our children want to relocate to the milder climates of Canada or Siberia?

Is humanity in the process of becoming able to see strangers as members of the same family? Can we have the conviction and commitment to consider our impact on the lives of others? Can we work together to solve shared problems? Will those who have resources waste them, unsustainably, while others suffer and die? Will too many choose to say, "I've got mine and that's all I care about?" If so, we will certainly go back to waging real wars of conquest over diminishing resources.

There is still hope. Our world is changing, growing, developing and maturing. The general tolerance of real war is evaporating. We are increasingly beginning to respond with brotherly consideration and liberal compassion for unknown others. Our sense of community continues to expand from family, to village, to tribe, to nation, to humanity, to all life on this earth. Are you truly committed to peace on earth and good will to men?

Targeted Drone Killing

We don't seem to have a problem with missile-armed drones here in central Iowa, but there are those among us who are worried about black helicopters coming for them in the night.

However, people in villages in other parts of the world watch armed drones circling overhead every day. Somebody (and anyone else near them) is probably going get blown to bits. There is no safe place to hide and there is no safe place for their children to play. That has got to get on their nerves. [Compare my short story "From a Distance," published in *Hubris on Roller Skates: Short Stories for Smart People* for another take on the subject.]

The rise of global terrorism has required governments to develop new policies and procedures. This is unlike any war that has ever been. It's not easy to wrap our minds around how things are changing. Lethal actions are no longer taken exclusively against nation states, but against widely dispersed groups and individuals.

Terrorist groups often gravitate to failed nations having inadequate rule-of-law, such as effective law enforcement and extradition treaties. Still, they pose real dangers to the security of the United States, its citizens, and to others who have the support of the United States.

Further, available technology has the capacity to multiply the massive damage that even a small group can produce. Imagine isolated tribes that are used to settling their grievances by ambushing individuals or shouting, throwing rocks and waving machetes. Now, imagine them gaining access to rocket-propelled grenades.

It boggles the mind. A radical religious militia might believe that non-believers deserve to die if they will not convert. With the help of technology, they could end up destroying an entire civilization. It has happened. Remember the effect of gunpowder and steel in the European conquest of the Americas in the 16th century.

Historically, military responses required the mobilization of nations, formal declarations of war, and occupation troops on the ground. As the technology of war advanced, the damage done to civilians became too horrible and unconscionable. Mounted cavalrymen gave way to tanks, rockets, aircraft, cruise missiles, bunker-buster bombs and nuclear weapons.

It no longer makes sense to firebomb an entire city when one can target training camps, convoys, and arms caches. Advancing technology allows combatants to produce increasingly precise damage with increasingly less risk to themselves and non-combatants.

Now, drones allow fighters to target individual buildings and vehicles. This seems considerably more restrained and humane than carpet-bombing larger areas. This new capability has tightened authorization-of-action procedures and combat tactics.

I haven't heard anyone point out that even municipal police may open fire on individuals that they (in their own judgment) believe to pose an immediate threat to others. SWAT teams may target those who pose a credible but less-immediate threat. We should recognize that drone strikes in otherwise-inaccessible areas serve to extend new technology into a gap in the continuum between law enforcement and war.

It comforts me to believe that our Commander in Chief inserts himself personally into reviewing intelligence and selecting terrorism targets. I would like to think that a Congressional oversight committee also has access to relevant intelligence and the ability to provide feedback, even if after the fact.

In the end, I expect that well-informed responsible parties will continue to adjust strategies and tactics while outlying left- and right-wing ideologues will continue to shout out their particular fears.

Understanding and Responding to Terrorism

Terrorism is a symptom of persistent social problems. It seeks to express resistance and create change by means of out-sized aggression. It uses "blind criminal violence" to motivate others to include the terrorist in their calculus of choices and behavior – or weaken themselves by reacting poorly.

Terrorism is usually a form of communication that is meant to produce powerful emotional responses. Whatever motivates any given terrorist, we are obliged to notice their act. Certainly, understanding terrorists' motives is vital to designing an appropriate counter-terrorism response. Terrorism is not a single-issue problem and does not have a single-tactic solution.

Several years ago, I had the opportunity to discuss terrorism with James Hippensteel, a professor of history in North Carolina. He startled me with an observation that I remember as: "Terrorism is the last resort of the desperate and impotent to gain recognition of their grievances and prosecute their struggle against a superior and overwhelming power." Dr. Hippensteel was careful to point out that he was not arguing that the use of terrorism was defensible but that, like smoke from a fire, it should be recognized as an indicator of an underlying unresolved issue.

Initially, I thought this "last desperate resort" observation on terrorism only applied to those who were oppressed and disenfranchised. These might include peoples experiencing genocide, slavery or subjugation. I thought of these as fundamentally *sympathetic* people, deserving *empathy and active intercession*. There are certainly many whose lives feel so hopeless that it becomes easier to choose to die than continue to struggle. And, why not die with honor, believing your death has meaning?

Eventually, it occurred to me that terrorism is also used by those who are very isolated and inflexible such as primitive tribes, authoritarian religions, and the politically indoctrinated. I thought of these people as deserving careful *nurturing* while they are encouraged to *learn* how to relate to their neighbors with greater *maturity*.

Later, I recognized that terrorists include some who simply seek to gain some advantage and have no compunctions about hurting others to get what they want. I think of these as sociopaths, deserving *contempt and active prosecution* to prevent their continuing aggression.

Finally, just when I was self-satisfied with my analysis and deconstruction, I realized that most terrorists fall under more than one of these categories. The world's problems are complicated and any effort to resolve them requires well-informed, nuanced, manifold, dynamic and flexible responses.

Terrorism Motives and Objectives

Further research finds additional perspectives on why some might choose terrorism. Let me regroup and offer this list:

A good day to die — What can you do when life, every day, is a desperate struggle with no hope of improvement? Even a sane person may become depressed and want to die. Nevertheless, they will prefer to spend themselves to die for a purpose. They will prefer that their death have meaning (if only symbolic) to their family and community. Everything else about deciding to die is subject to the vagaries of belief, circumstance and opportunity.

Dying with honor — One's belief system may honor martyrs. (Compare John 15:13, "Greater love hath no man than this, that a man lay down his life for his friends.") In fact, most religions teach that the faithful will be rewarded in an afterlife. Prospective martyrs also consider the honor and other benefits they expect to accrue to their name and family. The communities of martyrs often generously support their surviving families.

Curiously, sacrificing oneself with honor goes straight to the top of Maslow's hierarchy of needs. Martyrdom immediately dissolves all further concern for future survival, safety and relationships. It requires the ultimate in self-mastery and guarantees the esteem of others. Self-sacrificing nihilation for a worthy cause becomes the ultimate expression of self-actualization — especially when no other expression seems available. And, what righteous person does not want to win the approval of their god?

Psychosocial immaturity — Increasing maturity typically improves our capacities to accept delayed gratification and to tolerate change and differences in others. The fundamental explanation for individuals and groups adopting terrorism is the impatience, absolutism and authoritarianism of immature psychosocial development. Psychiatric studies attest that terrorists are not collectively insane or irrational; they are just poorly equipped to behave civilly. They own a hammer and every grievance is a nail.

A *first* resort? — Some researchers have observed that terrorism in Western Europe "tended to appear from the very beginning of the protest cycle." Terrorists often neglect to pursue viable political alternatives at the start. They also usually fail to embrace (or overtly boycott or sabotage) non-violent political activism when it becomes available. Totalitarian states (which would seem to be the most oppressive and protest-worthy) are the most effective at suppressing terrorism.

Oddly, however, terrorists often strike at open societies where peaceful non-violent political activism is more likely to get results. The evidence is that terrorists simply have a deeply held preference for violence that is stronger than their desire to actually remedy their expressed grievances.

Religious fanaticism — Throughout recorded history, religion has been a persistent source of violence. Fundamentalist-on-fundamentalist conflict is especially pernicious. When a group believes god is on their side or, especially, that god has blessed (or directed) their violence, they can justify almost any aggression. In fact, religiously oriented and millenarian groups tend to produce the highest levels of casualties;

willing to sacrifice their own lives (often with the expectation of a blessed afterlife).

Fundamentalists often believe they act out of moral duty and that their victims deserve death. Their attacks often target symbols of competing religious groups such as missionaries, funerals and houses of worship. Even seemingly minor variations of belief may trigger extreme prejudice. There is little to be done to remedy such behaviors except to encourage the development and embrace of more-developed worldviews.

No possible compromise — Terrorism tends to arise from peoples harboring authoritarian, absolutist, intransigent belief systems that are not open to negotiation or compromise. Their actual political positions are not always extreme, but their chosen means are. They will tolerate (and even stimulate) a protracted deadlock before accepting a partial win with a platform for negotiating further change.

Flexible focus — In order for a terrorist organization to persist, it must be able to fluidly identify new enemies and opportunistic grievances as changes in circumstances, societies or membership resolve old issues. Certain levels of worldview simply require concepts of absolute good and bad (with a defined enemy to resist, fight or even annihilate). In some circumstances, this worldview effectively promotes survival. Too often, it is a vestige of persistent delinquent development.

Strategic indifference — Terrorists often fail to make policy demands before (or even take credit after) an attack. They are squandering opportunities to harness their actions to an objective. Terrorists thus appear to focus on violence disengaged from, and indifferent to, any coercive purpose.

Intramural fratricide — Terrorists also often lose focus on external objectives and redirect their hostility toward related groups with similar policy platforms. This also reflects a focus on competitive violence over tactical purpose. Violent gangs provide the same environment of membership exclusivity, pride, intolerance by their attempts to generate respect through aggression. Cynical observers are left to shrug their shoulders in confusion and suggest, "Let God sort it out."

Personal importance — We all seek meaning and purpose in our lives; simply surviving is not enough. Acceptance and activity in a group provides a sense of belonging and value – subscribing to the shared story and receiving the embrace of fellow believers. One can be persuaded to do almost anything to avoid being put out of tribal fellowship. Urban gangs are a typical example of greater societal environments limiting personal options.

Conservative membership cohesion — Individuals within conservative groups typically embrace the dogma and ethics of that group. In fact, they tend to do so with the certainty, faith and self-sacrifice of classic tribal true-believers. They see such faithful commitment as a virtue. Such groups tend to collect around strong authoritarian leaders. Compliance to conforming behavior is an implicit factor of their continuing self/group-identity. Their membership (with its requisite compliance) gives their life meaning.

Some terrorist groups continue to be active long after they have achieved their objectives their ostensible purpose has passed. They may adapt new beliefs and goals to retain their group identity. They may even fight against indistinguishable alternate groups having identical goals. Sometimes, their motivation is more about belonging than achieving a specific end-point. The violence gives identity, meaning and a feeling of purpose, regardless of any actual purpose.

Attacking dissimilar groups — The powerful conviction of conservative membership groups easily translates into "we are right and you are wrong." This attitude may extend to "we are God's true people and you are agents of Satan who need to die." This can apply to differences in dogma between seemingly similar sects or large differences between social philosophies. Such animosity between competing groups can apply to race, national origin, sports teams, and much more.

There is no easy cure for such conservative group-identification. Explained elsewhere, breaking free requires a *personal* realization that one also belongs to a larger, more-diverse group, which transcends into an enlarged concept of "we." Such an individual's worldview expands to cope with greater complexity than their previous belief system explained.

This increasing personal tolerance for diversity is achieved with great difficulty. Because psychosocial development produces a discontinuity, each person who advances to this threshold easily becomes an unfit lured-to-sin apostate in the eyes of their former group members.

Attacking outside authority — Secular attacks for political issues often target specific symbols of established governmental or economic power. These targets may include banks, business installations and government offices. These attacks may embarrass or weaken the existing authority.

Destroying facilities may damage an organization directly or provoke it to over-react, expend resources or withdraw. Citizens may fear that their government can't or won't act effectively to protect them or their interests. Soldiers may abandon their posts and uniforms.

Hatred of freedom and democracy? — Some have claimed that anti-western terrorists simply "hate our freedom and democracy." Although this may contain an element of truth, it is a ridiculous oversimplification. Typically, conservatives of all stripes tend to be put off by the liberties and permissiveness tolerated by those who are more liberal. When you believe that God has established fixed standards of morality (but others flaunt that morality and seduce those like you into vile lives of intolerable sinfulness), liberality would, admittedly, be off-putting. Now, add acts perceived as greedy to brutal interventions by a disrespectful and hypocritical international super-power and you've got game on.

Retribution — Many terrorists, explaining their actions, point to the misdeeds committed by some entity represented by their targets.

Middle-eastern terrorists often talk about economic exploitation, military occupation, or moral corruption by/of foreigners. Timothy McVeigh (the "Oklahoma Bomber") was offended by the actions of American law enforcement agencies against members of militant religious and political movements.

Domestic actors — Homegrown terrorists have conducted numerous attacks on American soil. Recent violent citizen-activists have had issues with both conservative and liberal causes (including abortion clinics, environmental exploitation, animal rights, white supremacy, Christian identity, civil rights, capitalism, taxation, secession, end-times, and more). One cannot help but be alarmed by the extreme rhetoric and weaponization of some self-styled anti-government militia movement "patriots."

Foreign sponsorship — Security organizations of some governments encourage, support, and initiate terrorist acts for political advantage. This terrorism is usually intended to destabilize a foreign government. Consider the training manual, *Psychological Operations in Guerilla Warfare* published by the CIA.

Hide and run — Terrorists typically organize themselves from within weak states that do not have the will or resources to deal with them under civil law. Terrorists usually do not act as native fighters against a foreign army. Instead, like the worst kind of criminals, they exempt themselves from being subject to community standards of law, dignity, rights and responsibilities. Terrorists must hide because they know what they do is universally wrong.

Pure hatefulness — Some violence and terrorism is committed for no particular reason beyond personal animosity, cultural hatred, or just perverse gratification. This can include initiation rituals, team hazing and bigotry.

Social mimicry — Some violence and terrorism is committed to gain the approval of peers or desired membership groups. Many independent acts of terror are modeled after the violence of popularized news, movie or gaming figures.

Attacking moral turpitude — Secular attacks for social issues often target specific symbols of what are considered by some to be moral corruption such as hotels, theaters, clubs and abortion clinics.

Coordination for impact — Attacks for political and religious issues are often targeted for holidays or commemorations in order to increase their impact. The terrorists increase fear by demonstrating their ability to attack at will or to coordinate multiple attacks. The attack is made more memorable by happening on a day (or in a place) that holds special meaning.

Opportunistic monetary gain — Terrorism may include discreet acts of extortion, kidnapping, or hijacking for ransom. Groups may steal money, supplies or equipment to sustain or arm their operations.

Economic advantage — This is in the sense of getting "the most bang for your buck" (pun intended). That is, terrorists are political utility maximizers; they expect that their economic and/or political gain (less their losses) is greater than what they can achieve with any other strategy.

Time compression — Terrorism gets immediate attention while social protests and diplomacy may require the persistent commitment from multiple generations to produced desired changes.

Force expansion — Terrorism allows fewer individuals to get attention where other groups may lack the organization, resources or courage to act together.

Message amplification — It is not uncommon for small groups to experience trouble having their grievances heard. This is especially the case when those in power feel that those grievances are illegitimate (or disadvantageous). Because terror events are dramatic (and relatively uncommon), they easily become media events, which amplifies the desired publicity.

Repeat what works — Anyone, in any endeavor, will be inclined to repeat what works. If targets and victims do not work very hard to make it difficult for terrorists to succeed, acts of terrorism will proliferate rapidly. This relates to the controversy about whether or not to negotiate with or pay ransom to terrorists.

Ability to adapt and change — People are endlessly creative. When a counter is devised for one tactic, terrorists will invent another. This type of direct oppositional confrontation will inherently escalate until one party is crushed. Even then, if the underlying issue is unresolved, a new conflict will eventually reignite.

Failure to adapt and change — Curiously, some terrorist groups have declined to "accept success" by participating in non-violent political alternatives to achieve their stated goals. It is also common for a group to not "accept failure" when it becomes obvious that what they are doing is not working. It seems the meaning in their lives is preserved better by conserving their identity than by accepting victory or defeat for their cause.

Counterterrorism Tactics – Methods and Options

Counterterrorism efforts try to recognize the motives, tactics and organization of terrorists and then work to undermine the perceived advantages or ease of committing terrorist acts.

Deterrence — Deterrence is as much a part of law enforcement as crime investigation and prosecution. Conventional law enforcement and intelligence services may monitor, investigate, infiltrate and disrupt terrorist organizations. Governments often organize special dedicated counter-terrorism efforts.

Enforcement — When illegal violence occurs, governmental rule of law may respond, investigate, and prosecute those responsible. Stable governments are usually organized to deal with a wide range of crimes ranging from public nuisances to organized crime.

Extra-judicial actions — Because terrorists may operate globally and outside the law, many governments feel compelled to respond with covert and preemptive actions against them. This response may include unilateral strikes and operations inside foreign territories.

Cut their heads off quietly — Terrorism springs from a conservative and authoritarian worldview composed mostly of followers and a few malignant leaders. Quietly "disappearing" these leaders creates disruption and weakness in their organizations. This is opposed to the tactic of noisily martyring these leaders, which recruits more followers. Of course, new leaders will appear, but the terrorist organizations are weakened in the near-term.

Vigilantism — Where governments lack the resolve or resources to prevent terrorism, citizens may become vigilantes – forming their own guard or militia groups. This represents a seriously degenerative backlash. Citizens should never have to feel compelled to come to the point of taking law into their own hands. On the other hand, vigilantism satisfies the same personal and social needs that tend to produce terrorism. It should not be surprising to see these twin heads growing together from the same soil.

Deny access to weapons — Those who act from parochial ignorance and intolerance often lack societal restraint. The lives of their enemies hold too little value and the value of their own cause may be inflated — such as by perceptions of divine mandate. They may be willing to use weapons that produce indiscriminate harm wildly out of proportion to their grievance. They should be denied access to such destructive technology. Such weapons of mass destruction should be generally deprecated in any case. Increasingly, weapons that can be precisely and selectively targeted are to be preferred.

Economic ineffectiveness — When negotiators refuse to offer concessions and media refuses to publicize terrorist acts, the purpose and advantage side of the equation of terror disappears.

Economic costs — Terrorism becomes less practical when it brings down economic sanctions or targeted lethal attacks on the heads of terrorist organizations and those associated with them. Terrorism can be analyzed in economic terms. Any organization that finds it too difficult to retain supporters will weaken or fail. This is as true for a terrorist group as it is for a new restaurant with bad food in a poor location.

Strategic Responses to Terrorism

Economic interdependence — Groups that trade fairly and liberally with each other have a built-in disincentive to damage each other.

Economic access and justice — When people finally resolve injustices (such as achieving dignity and economic and social parity in their societies) their cause for complaint may rapidly dissipate. Frankly, this is a powerful argument for trade (and other) treaties that serve to reduce the gaps between privileged elite classes and the intractably disadvantaged. [*Sentiments like this are often taken to promote political philosophies that posit equality of outcomes. I mean nothing of the kind. I mean to promote greater justice in access to opportunity.*]

Social relationships — For millennia, leaders have negotiated marriage relations for the sake of peace. It's harder to attack each other when you might hurt members of your own family. Leaders have also deliberately dispersed conquered peoples throughout their existing domains. They expect that once people learn to tolerate (and even adopt) elements of each other's recipes, holidays, languages, and religions, this assimilation will reduce hostility.

Defuse regional, racial and religious bigotry — As a corollary, isolation promotes bigotry, suspicion, and hate. Groups that only communicate within their own "echo chamber" may learn to believe the most extreme falsehoods. Neighbors may even be perceived as less-than-human or too-sinful-to-live. Exposure to diversity gradually produces acceptance of diversity. This is a good thing, overall, but it really bothers existing bigots.

Take national action — Terrorism is a problem that cannot be adequately addressed at the individual, community or state levels. Even national governments are challenged to respond adequately. Terrorism will find us where we are and will wait for us where we go. Both Libertarian isolationism and Tea Party privatization will damage America's necessary federal responses.

Collaborate with other nations — Countries that share stable frameworks for civil society and the rule of law often cooperate successfully to discourage the organization of terrorist networks and prevent acts of terrorism. It is desirable to respond to terrorism with conventional law enforcement systems whenever possible.

International interventions — Some popular fiction supposes the action of a secretive international counter-terrorism response force. This is either an entertaining fabrication, a realistic option, or a covert reality. Take your pick.

International justice — Most terrorism is targeted against religious and/or social issues instead of specific countries. It has been suggested that an international court should be established to authorize action and render justice within the scope of this international problem. Coordinated international pressure could also be organized to dissuade countries that willingly harbor terrorist organizations.

Just kill them — The less-sophisticated your outlook, the more attractive you will find the option to simply annihilate the opposition… or even the *potential* opposition. The "Bush Doctrine" of unilateral preemptive self-defense against entire nations demonstrated a profound lack of subtly. President Obama's use of covert operations and targeted drone attacks at least attempts to dramatically limit the carnage.

Killing people without the benefit of a trial has been an accepted part of war for all of recorded history. However, it creates enduring resentments and is best used sparingly. Nonetheless, when others demonstrate that they are out to indiscriminately kill us (and those we are responsible for), it may be necessary, as a provisional tactic, to take the fight to them. Unfortunately, this is precisely the argument made and the motivation claimed by many terrorists.

I feel it is wrong to call terrorism "modern warfare." For one thing, the term "war" should be reserved for military conflicts conducted between nation states. Historically, many wars were winner-take-all affairs conducted expressly to plunder land and other resources. More-recently, more-limited wars have been waged for more-limited objectives of security, control and economic advantage. Increasingly, national combatants are expected to target military objectives while trying to exempt civilians. On the other hand, terrorists deliberately and explicitly target civilians. By contemporary standards, this is a very bad thing.

Attrition — Frankly, violence against citizens rarely achieves any viable purpose. It doesn't work. This fact doesn't seem to matter to existing groups who struggle to remain active – despite success or failure. However, with persistent counter-terrorism work, fundamental remediation of grievances (and without a history of success), the attraction to terrorism should eventually run out of steam.

Look to the future — Killing extremists who are willing to use short-term and desperate tactics, is, itself, a short-term and desperate tactic. Cultivating societal justice and access to opportunity will promote mutual tolerance and trust – a necessary and much-more-promising long-term strategy.

Unfortunately, climate change is already producing the same kind of regional distress that gives birth to new terrorism. Terrorism's short-term reaction to local grievances may be expected to out-run long-term global strategies to equalize opportunities for quality of life.

This difference in strategic vs. tactical time horizons elevates the urgency of global commitment to dramatically reduce the sources of climate change and create effective interventions to support those being harmed. We must anticipate the needs of all manner of refugees.

Look for the positive — The management technique of "Appreciative Inquiry" seeks to supplement the usual effort to reign-in out-of-parameter situations with a focus on discovering and reinforcing desirable behaviors, practices, and interventions. Finding what is good in other people improves our own attitudes while allowing us to express our appreciation and gratitude to others. This can become a self-reinforcing positive cycle.

Wait it out — Terrorists claim that they are trying to achieve specific policy objectives. History shows that acts of terror against civilians reliably fail to achieve their stated political ends. In fact, the public opinion and political consequences of using terrorism are usually negative. Citizens and governments typically become less willing to bargain with (or grant concessions to) terrorists.

Terrorism, as a strategy, is less than a failure; it is often counterproductive and thus irrational. About the only *desirable* result, from a terrorist's point of view, is that feelings of insecurity provoke liberal populations to elect conservative hardline governments. Unfortunately, such repression by authoritarian governments contributes to further grievances, which produce a self-reinforcing downward spiral that invites the growth of groups organized for reactive violence.

Change the paradigm — The only effective strategic response to terrorism is to resolve the underlying issues. Obviously if the problems were easy to remediate, they would have already been solved. Nonetheless, as long as the core conflicts persist, no tactic will succeed; defiance will continue to erupt.

Terrorism is not rational; it is a primitive emotional response. It springs from the persistent inability of a society to satisfy the survival, emotional, and spiritual needs of its members. It is a natural and normal anger response to chronic stress and misery with feelings of impotence. It springs from the extreme end of the same ubiquitous fountain as crying or complaining.

Unlike some well-organized popular revolutions and guerrilla campaigns, terrorism does not work and it doesn't seem to matter. Terrorism will never be eradicated; it can only be moderated and mitigated. It resembles an independent activity more than a coordinated project.

Promote spirituality — The highest, most-honored, spiritually-realized among all religions tend to retire from confrontation and emphasize individual harmony and loving self-sacrifice. Such spirituality promotes awareness, self-control, contentment, compassion, gratitude, tolerance, patience, peaceable relationships, universal brotherhood, and nurturing love.

Immature psychosocial development insists on grasping after short-term gratification and fear of (and pride in) differences which produce escalating conflict between groups. Maturity develops strategic patience and tolerance that springs from a sense of oneness with others. The more-broadly spiritual maturity can be practiced and promoted, the more peaceable our world will become.

Wisdom — No one can expect to succeed reliably without cultivating wisdom. In order to solve any problem, it is necessary to understand what is going on. The understanding and solution to any problem must exceed the complexity of the problem; this is especially challenging as our world rapidly becomes more inter-connected and complicated.

Sincere interest leads to knowledge of situations, relationships, constraints, beliefs and meanings. This, in turn, permits an informed response. Persistent effort allows for experience with success, which produces understanding. Persistent success is the hallmark of wisdom.

Solving relationship problems becomes especially difficult when some participants lack the 1) maturity and wisdom to recognize and understand the underlying issues and relationships and 2) the capacity to accept potential solutions.

Summary

Terrorism is a predictable social response produced by the conjugation of:

- an individual's and/or community's struggle to find meaning in life. This struggle is often related to frustration with limits imposed by circumstances and society.
- a conservative worldview that seeks the acceptance, approval, certainty, and control of group membership.
- an identified grievance with a clearly-defined enemy to blame.
- malign authoritarian leadership.

The primary solutions to terrorism include:

- making the world a better place so that it becomes easier for all people to lead productive and satisfying lives within communities of meaning.
- education, communication, and socialization that promotes expedited progress through stages of psychosocial development.
- undermining or eliminating the influence of individual authoritarian leaders who promote indiscriminate violence.

Terrorists should care that what they do is not very nice and makes it more difficult for people to like them and invite them over to play table games.

Terrorism is dishonorable and those thugs who commit it forfeit their dignity and any respect they might have earned for their cause.

Like stealing in the market, violence is easier than the alternative; it is the choice of those who are too lazy, impatient or cowardly to work at cultivating change in their own hearts, communities and societies. Terrorists squander the moral authority to make their case in the courts of law and public opinion.

Fighting Shadows and Doubts

Thank you to those who told me that they missed my columns during the last few months. [Summer, 2012, ed.] We were getting into the last convulsions of some very bitter political campaigns. I felt strongly tempted to respond to the upwelling of political partisanship by fighting a battle of ideas in print. Lord, some of those letters to the editor got me steamed. Instead, I put a bumper sticker on my car that said: "You are entitled to your own opinions, but not your own facts."

I almost got sucked into arguing with the undoubting faithful from the other side. That has variously been compared to "confronting a shadow in a knife fight," "grabbing the ears of an angry dog" and "throwing pearls before swine." Nothing good can come of it.

On the other hand, I believe we should persistently doubt our own assumptions, opinions and preconceived notions. It's like I used to tell my boys, "It's okay to talk to yourself and it's even okay to argue with yourself, but when you start to lose those arguments, it's time to start asking new questions."

During my years as a father, I began to doubt, more and more, some of the things I had believed for so long, and had spent so much effort to convince my boys were true. Take religion for instance. I taught them that there is only one true God – all-knowing and all-powerful. Therefore, there is only one true religion and one true truth – and, of course, that true truth was the one I believed. Faith is such a wonderfully certain thing.

However, the more I studied to defend my faith, the more I discovered other people with similar faith in their own true truths. In fact, I discovered that my forbearers had believed in a wide variety of similar, but vitally different, true truths, and that my peers in the same faith actually held a considerable variety of true truths.

The more I explored, the more I realized that, in all of recorded history, as regionally-isolated peoples discovered each other, they routinely exchanged language, customs, technology, tastes in food, clothing styles, and spiritual beliefs. As generations come and go, our faiths, like our habits, are fickle.

I eventually recognized that many things could not be known with certainty but must only be taken on faith. I began to prefer ideas where I had been persuaded by increasing evidence. Further, I became more careful to distinguish between things I took on (provisional) faith and on (accumulating) evidence.

We should all be alert to 1) doubt our most narrow prejudices, 2) be open to wider experiences and ideas, and 3) be ready to exchange outdated notions with new ones that do a better job of explaining our observations. When black-and-white fails, we should consider thinking in shades-of-gray. And, when that fails, we should consider how color serves us to explore ever-more-complex explanations.

There can be great comfort in belonging to a community of like-minded folks who share a common and non-threatening culture. However, when events change our environment, it will be courageous individuals who first scout-out how things are changing and explore how the rest of us can adapt so as to continue to thrive. These are not necessarily bad people or better people; they are just different. In fact, by figuring out how to bend, they show their communities, in difficult times, how to not break.

Positive Personal Emotions

Traditionally, psychology has focused on identifying and treating mental disease. However, the new field of positive psychology can help us identify and cultivate personal strengths so as to pursue happiness and enjoy positive emotions. This constructive outlook frees us from heavy burdens of regret for our past, unnecessary sadness in our present, and fear of our future.

Many people spend too much time entertaining sorrow, blame, and guilt over events from their past. However, the past is unchangeable. All we can do *now* is contemplate the past, learn from it, accept our present situation and decide how we intend to move on. Consuming ourselves with negativity is never productive. If we want to be able to forgive others and want others to be able to forgive us, we must start with learning how to accept our own forgiveness.

The present is what we have. Right now, we can experience this moment, interpret it for better or worse and make a choice. We can be happier if we act virtuously – in harmony with our values. Many people have realized that acting out of harmony with their values produces a lot of unnecessary stress. This can contribute to their load of guilt (or fear of getting caught). Granted, it may not be easy to resist pressures to do things you don't believe in. But, repeated decisions to do the right thing will begin to lock-in virtuous habits.

Is there any benefit in not trying to be pleasant at every opportunity? Smile at people with sincerity and warmth and they are more likely to smile at you, accept you or help you. We all prefer our present moment to be pleasant. But, our experience of the present is affected by more than just how others behave toward us. When our vital needs are satisfied, it helps if we can be content with what we have, without jealousy or covetousness. This kind of contentment is a blessing of satisfaction, appreciation and happiness.

There are certain things that people desire enough to be called needs. Satisfying each level of need increases our ability to be happy.

Obviously, we need to sustain our lives now and will usually do what is necessary to survive. For instance, having enough air to breathe is a good start. We desperately want security from danger and deprivation; we are capable of doing desperate things to obtain food, shelter and safety.

Beyond immediate survival, we are unsatisfied without a close relationship with others and having a sense of group belonging. We feel a profound deficiency when we are at risk or without reliable friends. We properly seek more than to just satisfy these deficiencies. We also seek self-esteem and the recognition of others. Ultimately, we are happiest when we can enjoy doing good, being creative, and expressing ourselves productively.

Our future can be powerfully influenced by the choices that we make, but much of our circumstances are not within our immediate influence or control. So, why waste time wallowing in fear? Choose to change what you can and accept the rest for now. People who deliberately involve themselves with others tend to be happier; they develop their social skills, interpersonal ties and social support networks; they experience more positive emotions; they are happier.

Positive Institutions

As Americans, the "pursuit of happiness" is an important concept. The branch of psychology called "positive psychology" introduced a focus on creating mental health. Positive psychology can also help us enjoy positive institutions. Of course, personal traits strengthen us as individuals, build character and help us to be happy. Positive institutions are also built on the strengths and traits of their organizing principles, their leaders, and others who are associated with them.

"Institutions" include much more than our schools, workplaces and governments. Families are one notable example of institutions. And so, we are actually talking about, not only family values, but the quality of all of the organizations to which we belong. We can also think of our cultural ideals of democratic group decision-making and personal access to free inquiry as institutional strengths that promote happiness.

Our personal character, values, strengths and virtues can contribute to our happiness in any situation. I recommend Viktor Frankl's book, *Man's Search for Meaning,* as an example of maintaining hope and even happiness under the most difficult and tragic circumstances. As another example, Helen Keller found a way to enjoy life, and contribute to the welfare of others, despite being blind, deaf and mute.

We are imbedded in the limitations of our environment, the cultures of our groups, and the interactions of our societies. Our circumstances play an undeniable role in our ability to survive, thrive and feel glad to be alive. It is easier to be happy when we routinely experience respect, justice, nurturing, good leadership and effective teamwork.

With positive enabling institutions, we can be more "drawn by the future than driven by the past." We can aspire to actually thrive rather than only survive. In fact, many people believe the proper and (vital) role of government is to not just protect its citizens from threats to their lives, but to also create an enabling environment in which they can be at liberty to pursue happiness.

Our embeddedness extends beyond our families and the ideal of competent parents nurturing their children. We depend upon our churches, civic organizations, schools, city councils, legislatures, executives and courts. Such organizations all contribute to our circumstances. Thus, it becomes very important to assure that our governing institutions have the resources and authority needed to fulfill their responsibilities to our safety and development.

Commercial enterprises, such as for-profit corporations, also have an impact on our safety and ability to thrive. Unfortunately, such companies are, too often, organized exclusively for private financial gain. Large businesses often promote their own profit and power rather than any need or benefit of other stakeholders such as employees and public citizens.

Our general welfare and happiness depends on governments being organized to protect their citizens from abuse. When governments grant undue privileges of profit, influence, power, and protection from accountability to the already privileged, it is just plain wrong.

Positive institutions, both private and public, are designed, managed and regulated to serve for good. They create good places to work and good places to live. Their activities protect from harm rather than create it. If we are to grant corporations privileges of personhood, we should also expect them to be good neighbors and good citizens. And, if we expect our public servants to serve us well, we should also expect to provide them with the resources and authority they need to do so.

Getting to Happy

The United Nations recently declared the first International Happiness Day. What's not to like about individual and general happiness? After all, our national culture is founded on an expectation of "life, liberty, and the pursuit of happiness." So, what can we all do to get happier?

One of the things that I learned, while working for Amoco Oil Company, was the management principle that "what gets measured gets done." The idea is that a leader must not only establish expectations, but create a way to measure progress and provide feedback to those who are responsible for, or affected by, the changes needed to achieve goals. (He or she must also find ways to reward those who promote that progress and punish those who obstruct it.)

The United States has used "Gross Domestic Product" (GDP) as a measure of economic activity since the Great Depression. Our measure of GDP has persistently improved; it has doubled since the 1960s. Yet, the economist who devised the GDP once warned Congress that "the welfare of a nation can … scarcely be inferred from a measurement of national income." Our focus on GDP may have contributed to so many capitalists focusing so exclusively on their own economic score card to the detriment of anyone and everyone else.

In 2005, the small Asian country of Bhutan began building and tracking their "Gross National Happiness Index" as a better alternative to pursuing only their GDP. It turns out that being happier both results from and helps produce better health, education, work, housing and governance. Bhutan's new emphasis is working for them and people are taking notice. What's not to like about gross national happiness?

And, this is not just touchy, feely, tree-hugging, new-age, liberal stuff. Since 1985, the formal business practice of "appreciative inquiry" has helped many organizations to make dramatic performance improvements by deliberately discovering what works best and then choosing to do more of it. Applying the psychotherapy technique of "unconditional positive regard" has helped many people to resolve relationship issues, be happier, and raise resilient, optimistic children.

An entire field of research has developed around "positive psychology." According to leading practitioner, Martin Seligman, "Positive psychology is primarily concerned with using the psychological theory, research and intervention techniques to understand the positive, adaptive, creative and emotionally fulfilling aspects of human behavior." Positive psychology is a refreshing complement to the traditional practice of waiting for something to go terribly wrong before intervening.

Positive psychology is not just for individuals. Seligman also explains that it is "the scientific study of positive human functioning and flourishing on multiple levels that include the biological, personal, relational, institutional, cultural and global dimensions of life." Positive psychology helps people learn to take better control of their emotions. They become more optimistic and actually succeed in taking responsibility for their future. Ideally, individuals are supported by an environment in families, schools and communities where fewer unnecessary obstacles stand in their way.

Our lives do not have to be "solitary, poor, nasty, brutish, and short." [Thomas Hobbes] Most of us accept that "God is love" and that by imitating His love, by cultivating the fruitages of the spirit in service to others, we improve the quality and happiness of both their lives and our own. It sounds to me like a great formula for happiness.

Living by Our Stories

The stories that we tell each other explain our world and give meaning to our lives. Our stories illustrate our cultural values and model our desired virtues. They teach moral lessons and set the foundation for our debates. Thus, we should think carefully about our chosen stories and beliefs.

When you were young, were you told to be good because Santa Claus knew if you were naughty or nice? Even the stories that we openly acknowledge as myths or fables are repeated to illustrate what we should or should not do and how we should relate to others. For instance, the story of *Pandora's Box* illustrates the bad that can happen from disobeying the instructions of someone older and wiser. Believing that thunder is the laughter of the gods can help ease a child's fear.

This week, Public Policy Polling (a highly ranked organization with a history of reliable results) examined widespread conspiracy theories sometimes held by American voters. Curiously, it turns out that those who identify themselves as 'very conservative' are usually more likely to believe any given conspiracy story. But, that's another story.

Consider these facts. "15% of voters say the government or the media adds mind-controlling technology to TV broadcast signals. An equal number are not sure. 5% believe exhaust trails seen in the sky behind airplanes are actually chemicals sprayed by the government for sinister reasons. 11% of voters believe the US government allowed the 9/11 attacks to happen. 15% of voters think the medical industry and the pharmaceutical industry invent new diseases to make money." These beliefs help explain widespread distrust of government.

It gets worse. 71% of people who called themselves very conservative say global warming is a hoax and 22% of those who voted for Mitt Romney believe that President Obama is the Anti-Christ. 11% of very conservative voters say they believe "shape-shifting reptilian people control our world by taking on human form and gaining political power to manipulate our societies" and another 10% are not sure. There does not seem to be any crossover data on whether President Obama is a lizard person.

Speaking of which, "29% of voters believe aliens exist and another 24% are not sure. 28% of voters believe in Bigfoot or are not sure. I'm not sure what any of this helps explain. But, it startles me to realize that, walking down the street, every fifth person I see may believe that our president is the antichrist or that some politicians are lizard people. I am even more startled by the thought: "What if they're right?"

What do our beliefs help explain to us (or about us)? How do our stories affect our values and choices in life? Do things happen for the reasons we have been taught to believe? Are there alternative explanations? If so, we should regularly give serious consideration to what we believe, what we value, what we do and why.

A New Story for America

Some stories that we tell about ourselves are constructive. Of course, we should want to be "the land of the free and home of the brave." On the other hand, ideas such as defending "the American way of life" may be destructive. Huh? What was that?

This old American way of life has involved the belief that "we're the best." Although it is a practical impossibility, you can still hear it at every team rally. It involved the belief that everyone is special so that every child in a group had to receive an award for something. It involved the belief that "we deserve the best" just because we are us. We spent decades being urged to put anything we wanted on credit; America was going to spend its way into prosperity. And then the bubble burst.

We used to believe that if you applied yourself in school, worked hard, married your sweetheart, bought a house and raised a nice family, then you could pay off your mortgage, retire and probably spend your golden years traveling. The people in charge were going to put a chicken in every pot, a car in every garage, and men on the moon. Science would keep on inventing, cure cancer and make everything better. Energy would be abundant and ever cheaper. We would face down communism and live on in peace and security. Well, it was a nice story and we made some good progress, but a few things about that story are due for some adjusting.

We should have seen that that story was too good to believe. We presumed that our exceptional success was our special blessing from an appreciative God. We believed that we could do no wrong. Instead, it turns out that many elements of "the American way of life" were selfish and wasteful; they were built on top of the exploitation and suffering of others and caused unsustainable depletion of national and global resources. Of course, it was a heck of a ride while it lasted. But now, we can begin to see the errors in that story. It's time to get real. It's time to grow up. It's time to be responsible.

We are in that uncomfortable act of reinvention between stories. Nevertheless, we still have the opportunity to pull together, invent and lead. Perhaps the greatest talent of Americans has been their willingness to come together in a crisis, embrace a common vision, and demonstrate the flexibility and adaptability to create something new and better.

But this takes a common vision, individual and collective sacrifice and plenty of hard work. Have we become too soft or uninvolved? Have our corporate interests become too greedy and shortsighted? Have we overcome "godless communism" only to fall prey to "godless consumerism" and personal indulgence?

Perhaps there is a better way. The original mission statement of the liberal organization "People for the American Way" began: "Our purpose is to meet the challenges of discord and fragmentation with an affirmation of 'the American Way.' By this, we mean pluralism, individuality, freedom of thought, expression and religion, a sense of community, and tolerance and compassion for others..." You're not against that, are you?

We still have a chance to believe in a better future... and to create it. It's a story worth telling. It's a story of "strengthening the common cords that connect us as humans and citizens" while we unite to work for opportunity and justice for all.

Perfecting the Stories We Tell Ourselves

We tell ourselves stories to give our lives meaning. This is how we know who we are, where we came from, what we should be doing, and where we want to go next. This is how we decide what is important and even what is real. Individuals, families, communities, cultures and nations may have different stories and so they hold different identities and expectations. The implication of this understanding about stories is that, when we change our stories, our realities, our lives, and our futures change too.

I was raised as a Kool-Aid kid; two cups of sugar and a packet of artificial colors and flavors made my world better. By the time I raised my children, they learned that "things go better with Coke," which could make the world "sing in perfect harmony." Children are now told that high fructose corn syrup will make them sick and shorten their lives. Did you know that New York City is banning large servings of sugary soft drinks?

In the earlier history of this country, settlers told themselves stories of magnificent destiny, glorious exploration, conquest and development. A continent of unbounded resources beckoned the adventurous with open land, virgin stands of timber, and even gold. They believed that one had only to keep looking forward, stake their claim and grow rich from exploiting abundance.

We believed that science, industry and reason would reform our animal natures as we designed rational Utopian societies. But, we now hear stories of declining resources, unintended consequences, heedless pollution, extreme partisan ideology, and unbridled grabs for unconscionable wealth and power. Science, industry and reason have become targets of criticism more than sources of hope.

In response to their fear, some people want to run away. They throw up their hands, abandon hope and retreat to dreams of individual autonomy and a story of God who loves them (and those like them) best. This is like retreating to a mother who will hold you, tell you that everything will be better, and bake fresh cookies for you; it is a comforting deception. Others want to fight. They hold up their guns and scream at any perceived threat. "I'll get my friends (or father, or bigger brother) and then you'll see."

What we need is a pervasive story of unifying community. In this story, our individual and family well-being is tied to our shared ability to cooperate – uniting to solve problems. Our advances in science, industry and reason are our newest abundant resources, not things to reject outright. However, modernity cannot lead us directly to a more perfect union. Only a more perfect civility can produce an improved civilization. This is the story we must tell.

It will not be comfortable, for a time, to live in a world of opposing stories. But, we need to dream of ways that every choice leads toward shared peaceableness and security for not just ourselves, but our neighbors and our world. We must be willing to extend our hands of fellowship instead of the muzzles of our guns. We have, at many different times, sacrificed so much for what we stand for. Who will tell our new stories? Who will stand up now to make their sacrifice of faith in the possibilities of our future?

Freedom and Responsibility

This week's *The Gowrie News* reported the winners of the 26th annual Fort Dodge Noon Sertoma "What Does Freedom Mean to Me?" essay contest. My family has been in a tizzy; we couldn't be more delighted. The first prize was awarded to Jaiden Ackerson, our eighth-grade granddaughter. Dianna and her daughter, Erin Ackerson, were able to attend the presentation luncheon today (March 7). This week, Jaiden is being recognized as a winner and a hero and has been modestly enjoying her recognition.

Instead of starting with a dictionary definition of "freedom," Jaiden led off by quoting Bob Dylan: "A hero is someone who understands the responsibility that comes with his freedom." She went on to say:

> "...freedom means living in a country where democracy matters, being able to have all races and religions peacefully live and work together, and being able to make personal choices while speaking my mind.

> "However, freedom does not give me the license to do anything I want, whenever I want. With freedom comes responsibility. Freedom allows me to make choices in my life, and those very choices come with consequences. These consequences may affect my life as well as the lives of others. When the consequences of my choices become negative, I may lose some of my freedoms...

> "Freedom is a privilege we must honor. Freedom allows all citizens to have the right to pursue an education of their choice, to work hard, and to succeed in their communities and their lives. We, as free people, also have a responsibility to protect our communities and the people who live there. This freedom spreads beyond me and my community. This freedom is so important to me that I must preserve it for future generations. The greatest display of appreciation for my freedom is to become the best individual I can be."

You don't have to fight a war or win a contest to be a hero. Our communities are filled with everyday heroes who simply accept their responsibilities and go about their lives taking care of what needs to be done. Some, seeing a need and having the capacity, extend themselves further and voluntarily accept additional responsibilities. Jaiden sees her mother not only managing her family, but as a nurse, also faithfully and lovingly caring for the weak and aged. Jaiden's grandmother went to college as an adult, became a teacher and served children in Fort Dodge and elsewhere for two decades.

It does not fall to everyone to be recognized for performing great dramatic acts. But our freedoms do allow us to make personal choices. We choose what responsibilities we care to undertake, and voluntarily contribute to the welfare of our families, communities, and our common good. As an example, I want to thank the nice neighbor who that took the time to coax my dog when it ran off, call the vet for my phone number, and then let me know where to find her. It was a pure act of neighborly care and civic responsibility.

Actually, taking on responsibility for something outside of ourselves is a choice to give up some personal liberties. Think of all the people who have given up time, attention and resources so that your life can be better. Parents sacrifice for their children. Volunteers sacrifice for their communities. Public servants should not be considered "takers" who are dragging down our economy. Instead, teachers, first responders, and even IRS auditors and EPA administrators serve our needs for learning, protection, fairness, and public safety. The have chosen to exercise their freedom to take responsibility for the good of others. They are our heroes and we should respect and honor them as such.

Is Social Psychology Best Left Unstudied?

The late U.S. Senator William Proxmire of Wisconsin criticized the work of two prominent social psychology researchers when he stated that, "Americans want to leave some things in life a mystery, and right at the top of things we don't want to know is why a man and a woman fall in love." Are there some things in life best left unstudied?

Proxmire, pork, and passionate prudishness

With all due respect, Senator Proxmire was a windy old curmudgeon who bragged that he was fired from his first job for impertinence and was fondly eulogized as being a maverick. His personal integrity, however, was reflected by a record 10,252 consecutive roll call votes across twenty-two years of public service. Proxmire took pride in lampooning wasteful "pork barrel" government spending and was notorious for giving "Golden Fleece" awards to many pork appropriations (with the notable exception of dairy supports in his home state of Wisconsin). The quotation, above, refers to his first Golden Fleece, which went for $84,000 given to the National Science Foundation in 1975 for the study of "Why a man and a woman fall in love." He should be forgiven a little hyperbole.

Under the circumstances, I whole-heartedly support Sen. Proxmire's position, at least to the extent that public federal funds, at that time, may well have been best committed to more-pragmatic needs. In any event, by 1975, a generation of beatniks and hippies had succeeded in establishing, to their own satisfaction, that spontaneous free love was better than traditional falling in love and marriage.

And, on that point, I'm happy to report that I fell in love with and married an ex guitar playing, protest singing, hippy chick. We are delighted with our commitment, as are a large number of aging ex-hippies and windy old curmudgeons like me.

I do not agree that falling in love is best left unstudied. I would be hard put to imagine anything (permitted by modern ethical review boards) that should not be fair game for scientific consideration. Curiosity leads to investigation, which leads to knowledge, which leads to wisdom, which leads to better personal decisions, which leads to better interpersonal relationships, which leads to better communities, which leads to better cultures, which leads to better societies, which just might, with any luck, save the world. That is what Social Psychology is all about, so let's rock on. Do I hear an "amen?"

On further reflection, the idea of scientists studying love has a wrong "feel" to it. The problem is not right out there on top and obvious, but there is a visceral alienness to the concept that makes one recoil from the proposition. It's like your adolescent child assuring you that if you let him take the cat apart he promises to put it back together again, or hearing someone explain the joys of peering at the starry heavens through the vacuum cleaner.

On the other hand, scientific study provides the rigorous analysis and differentiation needed for deep understanding and rational decision-making. For instance, we know that there are different ways of looking at things. As an example, pronouns can be singular, plural, indefinite, relative, and more, but who (but Ms. Thompkins in Senior English) really cares to formally sort it out?

Actually, it often helps to sort things out systematically. Follow me; this is going somewhere. Consider dividing our ways of looking at things into internal and external points of view and also dividing points of reference into singular and plural:

> **Internal/Singular** (I/S) refers to "*I*"–everything about your internal subjective experience of yourself including your feelings, thoughts, sensations, emotions, values, and opinions.

> **External/Singular** (E/S) refers to "*It*"–everything about one's objective observations of his or her environment. These observed objects can be measured for quantity or quality. This is the singular domain and the focus of science.

> **Internal/Plural** (I/P) refers to "*We*"–everything that the group you identify with holds as true, just, and beautiful. This is the

place of families, villages, tribes, and nations—as far as you have expanded to identify as "like me." This is the area of culture.

External/Plural (E/P) refers to *"Them"* or *"Its"*—everything that is outside of what you identify as "like us." This is the area of societies. We somehow have to get along with groups that are not like us.

Now, sex, love and romantic relationships form a very messy hybrid concept that spreads out through all four of the above quadrants. It is a strange and wonderful, dynamic; it develops and operates in additional dimensions beyond these four starter quadrants.

I/S includes your breathless wonder, and compelling desire to give.

E/S includes the sight of the sun sparkling in their hair and the fit of your lips when you kiss.

I/P includes your group's attitudes about appropriate matches and standards of beauty.

E/P includes how you're going to get along with your partner's crazy relatives such as uncle Larry, just back from fifteen years living with penguins.

On the other hand, science wants to look at and measure things that are isolated and well-defined. The ideal experiment reduces its observations down to a single independent variable. If a system is too complex, science will tend to invent a simpler model or look away altogether. By the time science has isolated the species of fungus growing on a tree's rootlets, it has totally lost its ability to observe the dynamics of multi-year rain cycles. Now, you want to use science to study social behavior?

I do, in fact, believe there is a place for scientific study of social behavior. Our Internal/Singular processes filter our senses through an unruly mass of previous experiences and interpretations. We tend to interpret new observations according to our experience. These mental filters frequently leave us incompetent to make consistently accurate private judgments.

The place of Social Psychology (as with science in general) is to inform our filters so that our everyday lives, including romantic relationships, can be conducted from knowledge rather than ignorance and prejudice.

Sure, we need to study why people fall in love, along with all the other aspects of Social Psychology. It's just that we simply need to be aware of the limits of scientific inquiry so we can choose to apply its revelations appropriately.

Writing in Iowa

Writing — really engrossing writing — springs from a rich and cluttered life, fully lived. It is the bounty of experience that loads the cannon of inspiration with sufficient shot to do memorable damage. But, can one glean adequate life experience from abiding among the ordered fields of Iowa?

Many an old Iowa farmer may be found breathing contentedly from the rocker on his back porch as he ponders the meaning of life, the vicissitudes of our mortal coil, the might of Jove and the recalcitrant whims of His weather. On the other hand, many an old Iowa farmer has been found moldering in the rocker on his back porch as the crows make sport with his remains.

But, back to the point. A connoisseur will cleanse his pallet before sampling a new wine. He will savor it, let it rest in the bounty of his experience and offer his judgment to enlighten others. An impoverished lush could not manage such a nuanced assessment. Likewise, critically acclaimed writers draw from the deep waters of their autobiographical wells. A dry well does not refresh. In fact, in Iowa, a shallow well, supplied by a groundwater aquifer, is likely to poison the family as they consume phosphates, organohalides, and fecal coliforms from the neighbor's hog operation.

But, back to the point. Good writing also requires clarity and order. For instance, I find myself unable to start a writing project if my desk is cluttered. I have to hide everything in drawers and boxes — putting it entirely out of sight — in order to begin. In this respect, the environment of Iowa is ideal for my writing. Iowa is an orderly place. I just open my window and gaze out at the regular rows of corn combing regular mile-square fields. The harvest is stored in parallel rows of grain towers spaced regularly along carefully aligned railroad spurs. Iowa spreads like a vast, bounteous cosmic checkerboard. I can stare out my window and not be distracted by anything but my aged widower neighbor and his crows.

But, back to the point. Not every writer cherishes an orderly desk or even an orderly mind. Some writers, such as the renowned Ray Bradbury, pride themselves on the stimulating clutter of their writing space. I do not trust this impulse. Bradbury described his writing process as being composed of two parts: throwing up and then cleaning up the mess. I do not trust that impulse either. Still, I suppose that Iowa supports that writing style as well. When I want to throw up, all I have to do is open my window and inhale the bouquet wafting from any of several animal confinements upwind.

But, back to the point. Iowa, commonly known as "the land between the vowels," has a long literary tradition. The *Iowa Writer's Workshop* has the reputation of producing the cream of the "crop." The workshop selects a "hybrid" mix of writers and poets who meet once a week for critical peer reading in Graduate Workshop courses. Of course, they may also meet for critical beer-sampling rounds. Iowa Pale Ale from the *Millstream Brewing Co.* at *Dave's Foxhead Tavern* comes to mind. Even writers can become connoisseurs.

But, back to the point. I love Iowa. I live in Iowa. I write in Iowa. Cluttered or clear, poetry or prose, fact or fiction, we've got a flock of fine folks here and I welcome you to join us. Just take care to cautiously keep clear of carnivorous crows.

[*Moving to Iowa seemed like a good idea at the time. But, as this book goes to press, my wife and I are preparing to move to the high(er) country of Southern Arizona. It turns out that she can no longer tolerate three-season allergies and I am having increasing troubles with the cold winters. We're gonna bail on Iowa and not look back. Maybe I'll write about that.*]

Citing Authorities

An on-line commenter recently suggested that my essays should "provide references supporting [my] presentation." However, I had not made an unattributed quote. Yes, I agree that writers should let readers know where an honest-to-god quote comes from. Nonetheless, this person seemed to want me to produce an outside-party authority for my personal beliefs and assertions. *That's* what blew my cork.

I responded that I'd given a great deal of thought to tracking the sources of ideas in my essays, articles and books. However, if one chooses to follow my columns and essays, they will see that I usually present the material as my own experience and opinion, which they (mostly) are.

The recent kerfluffle over plagiarism in Rand Paul's office really brings this issue to light. I agree with the pundits who say he should have given an attribution for many of his large copy-and-paste incidents. For myself, I am a lay searcher-for-understanding. Everything I have ever heard, read, watched or dreamed becomes grist in my mental mill so that my thoughts become my own source.

Yes, I sometimes work with a book or web page open in front of me. I will sometimes lift a particularly apt and irresistible phrase and put it in quote marks without attribution. I might briefly quote a few sentences from a source and name the author or work in the text. I have occasionally taken the liberty to produce a digest summary (condensing to about one tenth of the original work) but have been very careful to indicate the specific source and the nature of the work.

Nope, I have decided to not try to find a supporting authority for every thought I decide to put down. Like those authorities, I expect to have sufficiently assimilated what I have consciously consumed so that I can be responsible for the content of my own products. If a few unchewed peas come through as still recognizable, I will just have to stand up and apologize.

While I'm on the topic, have you ever thought about the ethics of writing about history that occurred before your own experience? It becomes patently obvious that every writer must, necessarily, derive all of their material from other writers (who probably derived their material from other writers) with no possible way of untangling the networks of thought sources.

In everyday life, we regularly use lines of reasoning, aphorisms, phrases and even individual words that were once original thoughts of someone else. But, once these expressions are recognized as sufficiently-apt, they are assimilated into our culture and everyday speech; no one expects an attribution.

Yes, in school, I was taught to cite my sources in research papers. I understood and appreciated the requirements for rigor in academic and scientific communications. I accepted the need, as an ignorant and dependent pup, to acknowledge the wisdom and primacy of my masters.

Now, as an old curmudgeon in my own right, I reserve the right to presume that my thoughts are my own. Please feel free to quote me on that.

Plagiarism

I own a fascinating collection of treatises on plagiarism in the volume *Perspectives on Plagiarism and Intellectual Property in a Postmodern World* published by State University of New York Press. Beginning on page xv, the Introduction makes the point:

> "Plagiarism is perceived as a problem but it is often discussed in simplistic terms: "using someone else's words without telling whose they are or where you got them"; "stealing other people's ideas or words." This basic view of plagiarism comes directly from the Latin source of the word, which meant to kidnap a person, referring only to children or servants or slaves: people who could in some sense be owned... A postmodern perspective of plagiarism and intellectual property suggests that one cannot own ideas or words. All we can do is honor and recompense the encoding of those ideas..."

I note (with considerable interest) that these editors, themselves, did not hesitate to simply enclose particularly apt phrases in quotes and move on.

Who owns the river as it flows past our fence? Do we hesitate to dip out what we need for our cooking pot or hesitate to piss back into the stream? Who owns the flow of ideas that constantly swirl and eddy through our literature and its many tributary media branches?

We cannot always know where our sources come from nor distinguish the edges with precision. Still, honor is due. I have a fading memory of accompanying David Winston, a Cherokee herbalist, on an "herb walk." As he crossed a small stream, he bent down, raised a few drops and touched them to his lips. He explained that the point of the act was to maintain an attitude of honor and appreciation for our resources.

My point is that some nuance applies to the subject. Most things cannot be accurately reduced to absolute binary alternatives. Still, I have respect for your fence; I will pay money for your bottled water, and I will not put your brand on the labels of my bottled water.

However, the movement of ideas cannot be constrained as if reducible to stone walls, heavy gates and monuments. The wind must, by its nature, blow through any crack. Rain will fall indiscriminately on any field. The resulting mass of water must find its way under, around or over any obstacle. Ideas must propagate like swirling wisps of dandelions, dancing on the breath of God, seeking new life in new places.

Blasphemy Incorporated

All opinions expressed herein by the author are offered without undue depths of rancor, malice, irony, or satire; only reasonably-balanced depths are intended. I name names and offer opinions but, any errors of fact are unintentional and sincerely regretted.

Today, I received several items in the mail, including a magazine subscription offer and a specialty mail order catalog. Both traded on themes of religion — especially Christianity. It did not appear that either company felt any need of remorse for their marketing choices. At first, I was tempted to simply discard the pieces as junk mail. However, considered together, they gave me cause to think about the nature of commercialism, American values and blasphemy.

The first item was an advertisement for "sinful savings" on subscriptions to *Free Inquiry* magazine (oriented toward the scientific examination of religion). I have a reputation for thinking (and writing) about such controversial subjects and wasn't surprised to be targeted by their mailing list. The envelope featured red blood splatters and the message, "Blasphemous! Look inside at your own eternal peril." They enclosed a "Special Introductory Offer – For Blasphemers Only." Also, "Your salvation isn't guaranteed... but your satisfaction with *Free Inquiry* is!" Their come-on letter starts, "Dear Intelligent Reader, You and I are under attack by religious fanatics who want to control what we read, how we think, and what our kids are taught in school. That's why they use words like blasphemous, godless and sacrilegious when bright, freethinking people ask questions that challenge their superstitious beliefs. These are words meant to inspire fear and intimidate the weak-minded into submission."

All of this seems like outright inflammatory sensationalism used for commercial advantage. These words, in this context, are also meant to shock, inspire fear, attract gratuitous attention and sell magazines. I actually admire the effective use of language to motivate *appropriately*. I admire the insights of Frank Luntz, a Republican Party Strategist and wordsmith, in how to use words and re-frame arguments to push people's emotional buttons. I just don't actually buy his doublethink inventions and arguments. Moreover, I just won't buy what might actually be an interesting magazine when it is promoted in this way.

However, the magazine advertisement also enclosed a note from Richard Dawkins (a renowned evolutionary biologist and outspoken atheist) saying, "If there were a God, I'm convinced He would want you to read *Free Inquiry*," adding, "He would be committed to the application of reason and encourage scientific discovery and the cultivation of moral excellence. He would want us to be more concerned about living a valuable life than enforcing arbitrary rules to avoid a vindictive punishment in an afterlife."

Richard Dawkins also pushes some emotional buttons: reason, discovery, moral excellence, valuable life and vindictive punishment. Did you notice how positive, reserved and respectful he was in framing his note? "God" and "He" are appropriately capitalized as honored divinities. Dawkins appeals to cultivating moral excellence and living a valuable life. You got a problem with that? I don't. You got a problem with exposing religious (or any other kind of) hypocrites and moral corruption? In the Bible, Jesus didn't. Still, I don't think Jesus would have subscribed to *Free Inquiry*. I imagine that He might have given permission to be quoted, but not been manipulated by their advertising.

My wife, Dianna, is a retired elementary school teacher and still receives catalogs from the "Oriental Trading Company." This issue featured "fun and faith" items with the exhortation to, "share the spirit." It contained a mix of holiday spirit and (evidently by allusion), "Holy Spirit" trinkets, gifts, activity packs as well as carnival and fund-raising prizes.

They obviously expected to sell profitably to those wanting to promote and commemorate religious holidays and classically fundamentalist Christian themes. I'd like to think that if they thought that certain items would be easily considered blasphemous, they would not advertise, stock, and sell so many. Note to self: "A clear conscience is no more a guarantee of rectitude than an empty head is a sign of intelligence."

First, let me acknowledge that I am a cranky old curmudgeon and some of you will think that I'm being overly critical. Any issue, taken by itself, may be easily excused. However, the catalog collection, taken all-together, represents a serious disregard of appropriateness and dignity among self-professed spiritual and faithful people.

The catalog cover features three young children, singing hymns in "angel costumes," complete with cheap white polyester gowns, battery-operated candles and white "feather and marabou wings." It is not entirely clear if real African Marabou Storks are "harvested" to produce these authentic-looking wings. That would be an entirely separate animal conservation ethics issue. Also, I want to suggest that it would be an easy mistake to dress your little cherubs in thin polyester and then substitute authentic candles, flickering with actual fire.

The vendor evidently also dyes marabou wings red to produce similar "Cupid wings." That ad reads, "Put on these feather and marabou wings and find true love as a matchmaking Cupid or use them for an angel costume on Halloween!" We have discovered an unholy amalgam of child-angels in heaven, Cupid, the Roman god of erotic love and the likely improvisation of a sexy fetish costume. It doesn't seem to matter to anyone but me. And further, I'm not too fond of Halloween as a festival-for-the-dead with little beggars dressed as angels, devils, zombies, pirates, and hookers.

Speaking of little angels, my wife's older brother died in tonsil surgery when he was seven. Her mother's pastor explained that God called her boy to be a little angel in heaven and that a bouquet of flowers also needs buds to be pretty and complete. Her mother evidently believed this literally and repeated it often in defense of the comfort that she claimed it brought her.

Nonetheless, she never escaped the obvious trauma and bitter desolation of her loss. She became an alcoholic and chain smoker and died prematurely of lung cancer. Don't try to tell me that a capricious and self-serving God exercises a prerogative to harvest little angels from our families to decorate his abode and sing eternal praises to his wonderfulness. Don't try to tell me that I should believe it too.

And, when did "Christ our Savior" start getting blithely mixed up with evergreen trees, snow men, a jolly old elf sliding down chimneys and other such nonsense? You can buy color-your-own Christmas nativity stockings; gingerbread, rubber ducky, and gnome nativity sets; nativity bingo and playing cards; "Happy Birthday Jesus" balloons, party hats, beach balls, kaleidoscopes, slide puzzles, novelty assortments and ornaments; "Jingle for Jesus" bell bracelets; nativity crosses (just a slight anachronism); plus "Jesus Loves You" and "Caleb the Camel" Christmas tree ornaments.

There is more. You can buy golden crown and "Jesus is My Rock" stress squeeze toys; "King of Kings" tattoos (hardly in the spirit of Leviticus 19:28 or Deuteronomy 14:1), favor boxes and treat bags; "Joy to the World" paddle balls; "Joyful in Jesus" candy canes, Bible verse fortune cookies, and "Testamints(tm)" breath-freshening candy; "Share His Light and Love" and "Jesus Loves You Snow Much" snowmen; "Jesus Lights the Way" flashing bouncy balls, "Bible Bucks" play money, and "Pick Jesus" guitar picks; as well as rainbow faith bears, "Our Wise Lord" owls, "Jesus is Deer to Me" reindeer and "Wild About Jesus" safari animals.

You will definitely want to proudly display your own Celtic Cross Bible cover (incorporating a pagan solar nimbus). What can I say? It appears that non-believers do not have the corner on impiety. A mix of ignorance, indifference, conceptual hybridization, and crass commercial blasphemy are popular (and big business) among religious "fun"damentalists these days.

All the time, I run across people who want to tell me that they know what the truth is — that they are in charge of explaining what (their version of) God wants everyone to believe and do. I can spot them right away; I used to be that kind of faith-and-fellowship true believer. Now, I can't imagine what makes them better than any other tribe of mere mortals with similar convictions. I am appalled, not persuaded, by the arrogance, presumption, and hypocrisy of their blasphemy.

Addendum:

I am continuously in awe of the cultural literacy of my wife, Dianna. She exposed a fondness for the pre-hippy beat poets and raging social critics when she recommended that I cite part of Lawrence Ferlinghetti's related poem, "Christ Climbed Down" from his book, *A Coney Island of the Mind*. It is a biting criticism of the commercialization of Christmas:

> Christ climbed down
> from His bare Tree
> this year
> and ran away to where
> no fat handshaking stranger
> in a red flannel suit
> and a fake white beard
> went around passing himself off
> as some sort of North Pole saint
> crossing the desert to Bethlehem
> Pennsylvania
> in a Volkswagen sled
> drawn by rollicking Adirondack reindeer
> with German names
> and bearing sacks of Humble Gifts
> from Saks Fifth Avenue
> for everybody's imagined Christ child

The NRA Speaks Out on Packing Heat

It may surprise you to discover that the National Rifle Association has recently strayed quite far from its traditional moderate views to embrace much more radical policies. For instance, the position of the NRA on carrying guns in public has changed over time.

Has the leadership of the NRA embraced the developing maturation of American social conscience, or have they been lured to pander to the interests of weapon manufacturers? I usually try to resist cut-and-paste columns, but I want to offer some cherry-picked quotations drawn from "academic histories of the NRA" for your consideration.

"I have never believed in the general practice of carrying weapons. I do not believe in the general promiscuous toting of guns. I think it should be sharply restricted and only under licenses." - NRA President Karl T. Frederick, praising state gun control laws when he testified in Congress before the 1938 federal gun control law passed.

"We do think that any sane American, who calls himself an American, can object to placing into this bill the instrument which killed the president of the United States." - NRA Executive Vice-President Franklin Orth in testimony to Congress, shortly after Lee Harvey Oswald shot and killed President John F. Kennedy.

"There's no reason why on the street today a citizen should be carrying loaded weapons. … [guns are] a ridiculous way to solve problems that have to be solved among people of good will." California Gov. Ronald Reagan (May 1967).

Ronald Reagan also spoke to Congress in favor of the Brady Bill's waiting periods and background checks: "You do know that I am a member of the NRA and my position on the right to bear arms is well known, but I want you to know something else, and I am going to say it in clear, unmistakable language: I support the Brady Bill and I urge Congress to enact it without further delay."

Also consider former U.S. Supreme Court Chief Justice Warren Burger (a Republican appointee), "To 'keep and bear arms' for hunting today is essentially a recreational activity and not an imperative of survival, as it was 200 years ago; 'Saturday night specials' and machine guns are not recreational weapons and surely are as much in need of regulation as motor vehicles." (January 1990) Also: "[The Second Amendment] has been the subject of one of the greatest pieces of fraud, I repeat the word fraud, on the American public by special interest groups that I have ever seen in my lifetime." (PBS "News Hour," 1991)

The closer we look at our passions of the moment, the more we tend to lose sight of the larger picture and greater context. Why do we vigorously defend the accepted wisdom of today's authorities as sacred writ without actually stopping to think about how our convictions developed or may need to change?

- Does arming as many citizens as possible actually protect more people from violence?
- Is America, with its gun culture, safer than other developed countries with tighter firearm regulations?
- Should potentially lethal items such as automobiles, medical devices and guns require special training, licenses and insurance?
- Should we be alarmed that the most-vocal defenders of "gun rights" are also the most vocal about being able to personally take "Second Amendment remedies?"
- If you saw someone carrying a firearm into your bank, would you be more likely to congratulate his patriotism and offer to buy him a cup of coffee or leave the building and call 911?

The attitudes now defended as inviolable truth are, in fact, the products of a dynamic and developing past. We should acknowledge that our society's future needs are also subject to necessary change. We should make it our mission to disengage our minds and hearts from hostility and aggression and our fingers from triggers.

Ref: "Gunfight: The Battle Over the Right to Bear Arms in America,"
Adam Winkler, 2011

Values, Virtues, Vices and Sins

I want to thank all of you who have followed my last few months of political commentary. We have especially explored the differences between those who are uncomfortable with change and those who can face it with hope as an opportunity to improve matters – those who fear the risk of losing what they have and those who have the faith to work with strangers to achieve what they cannot do by themselves.

Values and virtues underlie our private and public choices. And, I want to move on to thinking about what makes us decide that something is good or bad and then choose what we will or won't do. This column is about to make a shift. I thought a little fair warning was in order. Here we go…

As we grow up, we are taught to conform to our families' and communities' standards of belief and conduct. We gradually develop a sense of right and wrong as we are taught what is good and what is bad. Yes, there are some values, such as not stealing or not committing murder, that seem "natural" because they are shared by so many different societies. And yes, we can see for ourselves, over time, how different choices tend to result in different consequences.

At the same time, even things considered sinful may otherwise be considered virtuous depending on circumstances. Take stealing and murder for instance. We rarely blink at stories of the God of Israel commanding His people to plunder their enemies and commit genocide as they came into their promised land. We routinely justify many of the atrocities of war when they are committed by "us."

Values are the opinions we hold and the judgments we make about what is good and bad. However, we sometimes do things contrary to our values. Further, our values may actually sometimes conflict with each other. But, even the most wonderful values are empty if they do not direct our choices and our actions.

Virtues and *vices* translate our values into our actions. There is no virtue or vice until we actually do (or choose to not do) something. Only after we make a choice and act can what we have done be judged (against those principles and values that we hold dear) as virtuous or not.

Sin is essentially falling short of the mark – failing to meet the expectations or model set for us by an established authority. Most often, sin is used in the context of failing to keep the commandments of one's particular God. Please remember that we live in a large, diverse and dynamic world where many different people worship their own God(s) with similar obedience, faith and devotion.

We should hesitate before expecting everybody else to conform to our personal values as the only possible acceptable values. This is especially evident when we consider that our personal values (or understanding of our God's values) will predictably change over time as we develop and mature.

Finally, we need to keep in mind that even non-religious people hold family, community and societal values. One way or another, we all have some basis for making choices; we all make personal judgments about what is good and bad. We should make the effort to understand our own thinking and to be aware of the values of others.

Debunking Trickle-down Economics

In 1896, William Jennings Bryan declared that, "There are two ideas of government. There are those who believe that if you just legislate to make the well-to-do prosperous, that their prosperity will leak through on those below. The Democratic idea has been that if you legislate to make the masses prosperous, their prosperity will find its way up and through every class that rests upon it." Later, Lyndon B. Johnson added, in his brutally blunt style: "Republicans [...] simply don't know how to manage the economy. They're so busy operating the trickle-down theory, giving the richest corporations the biggest break that the whole thing goes to hell in a hand basket."

This economic idea of "trickle-down" dates back to the earlier horse-and-sparrow aphorism: "If you feed the horse enough oats, some will pass through to the road for the sparrows." In our time, it was formally called "supply side economics." Ross Perot called it "political voodoo." Whatever you call it, it has been a dominant political policy priority in many governments and corporations for a long time. But, a metaphor producing an easily-visualized image does not make it an apt model of reality.

So, how have we sparrows been doing down here under the back end of the horse? In 2012, a European taxation research group concluded that: "...wealth of the super-rich does not trickle down to improve the economy, but tends to be amassed and sheltered in tax havens with a negative effect on the tax bases of the home economy." Oops, that's not so good.

The common philosophy of favoring those who need it the least saturates the entire history of wars of conquest, colonialism, slavery, unfair trade treaties, predatory loans and exploitation of others' resources. Remember that our own nation's origins lie in our rebellion against colonial exploitation. This view of things completely reverses the Ayn Rand idea of who are "takers and makers." Consider substituting the concepts of "privileged elite" and "working poor."

How should our nation treat lesser-developed countries who may view us as the exploiters? While some economic inequality is inevitable, the politically powerful and prosperous do well to remember that hoarding their ill-gotten gains while others suffer in abject misery just doesn't look good and isn't very nice either. It didn't work for the thirteen American colonies in 1776 and it still triggers opposition to "economic imperialism" now. I'm reminded of George Monbiot's comment that, "If wealth was the inevitable result of hard work and enterprise, every woman in Africa would be a millionaire."

How does it make you feel to know that people working full-time at your favorite stores are still in poverty with no practical path up? How does it make you feel if you're the one working full time and still dependent on government aid? It makes me feel like some corporations have found a way to get the government (substitute "taxpayers like you and me") to subsidize the low wages and benefits that they make available to their employees. That isn't very nice either.

I do not believe that we all deserve equality of outcome. But, what we do owe each other is equality of opportunity. We all expect dignity, justice, and a fair chance. Growing inequality inevitably produces social and political instability. These truths have been borne out by thousands of years of struggle for survival, social progress and spiritual attainment.

A New Democratic Strategy

The bottom line is that Democrats should stop engaging the far right as equals. Groups such as the Tea Party are not actually mainstream. Their ideology continues to move so far to the right that it is becoming difficult for many Republicans to defend it. We should stop trying to meet them on common ground. You cannot negotiate with someone who holds extreme views and will not compromise. You cannot reason with someone who is unreasonable.

We should stop treating radical ideologues like equal and rational opponents. We debase our ideas and ourselves when we invest our energies in point-by-point name-calling, finger-pointing and obsessive refutation. Worse, by meeting our opponents as responsible peers, we elevate and amplify every lie and damaging policy they mention while signaling their legitimacy. Because they do not expect themselves to be factual, or even consistent, they have mastered the art of twisting language, re-assigning meaning, and persuading the already-faithful with loud voices and repeated talking points.

Imagine a street preacher, shouting to the wind. Imagine the insane raving to their padded walls. Where is the benefit of engaging them as equals? What is the value of giving what is holy to dogs or of casting pearls before swine? When pushed, the radical-right base will only double-down their defensive loyalty. Their base will not be moved just now. These followers will have to see their authorities repeatedly humiliated, ignored and impotent. No amount of appeal to reason will suffice. It is time to lead forward.

Many in the American public fail to differentiate between the noise and confusion of the opposing campaigns. To them, it's beginning to sound like two primitive tribes, screaming incoherently, and throwing rocks and feces at each other. It is an entertaining spectacle for a short time, but not inspiring. Neither group succeeds in distinguishing or elevating itself.

The Democratic Campaign needs to quickly define and seize the virtuous, emotional and intellectual high ground, rise out of the dust, and reframe debate in terms of liberal values. We must not allow the "better angels of our nature" to be drowned out. Without clearly defining and claiming our virtues, a vast swath of our neighbors will turn away in despair, muttering "a curse on both their houses."

You see this generalized alienation and indifference all the time and it is growing… and it is a golden, low-hanging fruit of opportunity. You see it in the hunched shoulders of some farmers as they go off faithfully, year after year, to tend their fields, but cannot be persuaded to attend their wives' churches. You see it in the empty eyes of some people, content to sit, hour after hour, to be entertained, but cannot be persuaded to become engaged in their communities. You see it in the endless hours that entrepreneurs will sacrifice to building a small business that might sustain their families now, but are too burdened down to look up, lock arms, and lead others to a better future.

The American People are not immune to fear, and our times are increasingly fearful and trying. There are several possible responses to fear and no one option is unavoidable or unchangeable. Some may withdraw into personal isolation or the protection of a group of others like themselves. Some may strike out at others who are not like themselves. Yet, others are able to face and transcend their fear. This growth to maturity and strength is an individual achievement, even when it is helped along in a nurturing and supportive environment.

In fact, this individual achievement, united in good works for a common purpose, is the core of the Progressive Vision. We aspire to put aside our fear with all of its baggage of selfishness, hate, prejudice and bigotry. We aspire to empathy, self-control and goodness. We have faith that living such lives will help lift our neighbors out of fearful despair. We believe that, by working together, communities and nations can solve problems that private enterprises can never address. We believe in individual and collective attention to the common good. Progressives (atheists and religionists alike) aspire to the law of love.

Where do you most see fear? You see fear in those who feel, individually and collectively, the most powerless to acquire or create what they want or need. It is natural, under those circumstances to avoid risk, to conserve and defend what you already have, and to seek out strong and authoritative movements and leaders. For some, religion serves the purpose of giving hope – if not now, then in the afterlife. Others see stockpiling wealth, arms, or private political influence as a source of security. Why should I name names? By their works, you will know them.

Perhaps it is an offensive metaphor but, the most loyal dogs have been rescued from the most abject and fearful circumstances. I believe that this principle explains the willingness of so many people in so many times and places act against their best interests. Lacking their own power, they seek authoritarian leaders – sometimes leading their nations to tribal fragmentation, fascist regimes or the impossible promises of "benign dictators." We must present a better way.

Happily, the cure for such fears precisely tracks the progressive agenda: A supporting hand up for those who need it; public education; improved general economic security; increasing engagement with diverse peoples and ideas; increasing individual participation in civic and social improvement projects.

The Democratic Campaign should still defend itself against the attacks that will inevitably be thrown their way. But, have faith; there are multitudes of progressive supporters who will gleefully throw themselves into the fray. They will take it as their duty and privilege to defend, protect and respond in support of reason, truth, insight and vision. They only need to unite behind clearly articulated purposes to give their work meaning.

The Campaign should continue to release current talking points, produce point-by-point explanations and authorize prominent surrogates to model desired responses. So armed and empowered, supporters will not just have your back; they will swarm in every direction in your service.

Above all, the Campaign should make clear the intellectual framework that underlies progressive ideas. And yes, it is useful to contrast and compare progressive values to limited and self-centered values. But, the point here is to repeatedly stimulate a sympathetic emotional response to the liberal morality and values that promote good will toward our neighbors. The opposition's selfishness, lack of empathy, and shortsighted vision will obviously lack personal and public value in comparison.

We should point out the cyclic pattern of commercial abuse and progressive response in the history of this country. Sometimes we forget about the public demands for such things as monopoly-busting and voting rights. The Republican slide to the right needs to be publicly exposed as a deliberate multi-decade effort to undermine our government's capacity to empower its citizens, protect them from private exploitation and increase general prosperity.

More specifically, the systematic efforts of the most-radical conservatives to increase their influence (from public school boards to the Presidency) is more than the usual political maneuvering. Conservatives were stung by their failures to maintain racial segregation and humiliated by the progress of social liberties including the further empowerment of women. Republicans have been engaged in a systematic counter-insurgency that was triggered by the Conservative Coalition's losing their battle against civil rights. To me, that makes today's politics *a battle against pure evil*.

We began noticing "ultraconservatives" and the "radical right" nationally in 1961. Multiple influences have contributed to the effort. These include the religious Moral Majority, the Koch brothers and networks of other wealthy businesspersons, conservative think tanks, and many large corporations acting through lobbyists and the American Legislative Exchange Council (ALEC). More recently, the Supreme Court allowed unlimited anonymous contributions to Political Action Committees. These common threads mark the increasing influence of private wealth in corrupting what should be all Americans' government.

Many of today's Republicans were more comfortable back in the days when both the Democratic and Republican parties had their liberal and conservative wings... and legislators were expected to represent their constituencies and vote their conscience. Many public servants in both parties are still motivated by a desire to establish a more perfect union and work for the public good. Not every conservative, and not every Republican, is psychically invested with the right wing's radical fringe.

Now, add the fact that the Democratic Party has moved so far to the middle that they have disillusioned some of their own "loony left," and you have a situation where they could appeal to a large number of independents and centrist Republicans.

There is hope. However, hope needs the clear light of effective communication and inspired leadership to prevail. We embraced that hope in 2008 and we're alert for that light and leadership to reassert itself, out of the noise and clutter, now.

Research: Does Conservative Negativism Repress Rational Thought?

Conservatives are fond of identifying "enemies" and using strong negative words and images to describe them. I wrote about this in the essay *Conservatives Depending on Emotional Words to Persuade* where excerpts of a GOP memo from Newt Gingrich suggest words to describe "our opponents" including: failure, pathetic, lie, liberal, betray, hypocrisy, radical, etc.

Psychologists have already discovered that emotions affect higher brain functions including attention, memory, vision and motor control. Now, researchers are discovering that negative language inhibits the lower level retrieval of knowledge and subconscious information processing. A Bangor University study initially expected that negative emotional words would be arousing and stimulate reasoning capacity. Instead, they found that negative words suppressed certain cognitive responses.

I suggest that combining these two observations may show that repeatedly describing liberals [or another race, or immigrants, or non-believers] in negative terms *may reduce the audiences' ability to reason critically about the information they are receiving.*

What do you think? Is this why so many people report that it seems futile to try to reason with conservatives? Does this imply that liberals should also decide to deliberately target the limbic (emotional) centers of any given audience's brain? Would that be unethical, too cynical for words, and against our "religion of reason?"

I don't believe that I'm rushing out on a wild tangent here. If you've been reading my essays, you'll recognize a greater context. I've reviewed Bob Altemeyer's book *The Authoritarians* where decades of research establish conservative modes of thought. I've described research into stages of human development that explain how we all, at some time, embrace a conservative worldview, based on the accepted beliefs of our group.

Some individuals, but not all, break loose from their limiting group identification through individual struggles to understand a broader context for meaning. These people escape the trap of defending "individual freedom" while they continue to conform to the teachings of their limited scope of associates. They discover the true meaning of individual freedom in being able to conceive of others also exercising those freedoms independently.

My point is that there is a growing body of evidence to explain the difference in reasoning styles between those with narrow vs. broader views – those who are comfortable accepting the militant and negative dogma of splinter-group authorities and those who have the courage to work hard enough to understand a larger view of how things are.

Negativity about others and fear of change need not be locks on our doors of understanding and opportunity. Get positive and have faith in the goodness of your potential and that of the world around you. If your way of thinking isn't working for you so much anymore, undertake the struggle to break out of your chains and see a wider world. There is always more. But, you'll never see it if you're content to be like just another puppy crawling over your litter-mates in a box.

Reference: Bangor University, School of Psychology, Centre for Research on Bilingualism; *Journal of Neuroscience* (May 9, 2012; 32(19):6485– 6489, 6485)

Jobs-Part 1: Automation

Whatever happened to all the elevator operators, telephone switchboard operators, cabbage pickers and tollbooth collectors? These and many thousands of other jobs have been eliminated by automation technology. On the bright side, we can now directly dial almost any phone in the world and not have to worry about watching our seconds on long distance calls. But, these are jobs, for you and your neighbors, that will never come back.

Our losing so many jobs to machines is not the end of the world or the end of work, but it is traumatic. The changing nature of work (and availability of jobs) will create some economic challenges. You see senior citizens sacking groceries when they would rather be holding their grandbabies or nursing their bunions. You see college graduates assembling grease-burgers (hold the ketchup) when they would rather be building their families and paying off their student loans.

We've gone through this before. Whatever happened to tanners, weavers, cobblers, and blacksmiths? Those were the days of craftsmen, apprentices, and hand-carved ornamentation on furniture. You could tell who had made a piece by the personal touches in its design. You took care of what you owned because you knew that years of experience, hours of labor and, sometimes, sweat and blood went into its production.

Brute labor gave way to water wheels, which gave way to steam engines, which reorganized economies and the nature of work around factories. Eventually, electrical motors replaced steam, but the factories never went away. At each stage, production efficiency increased and standardization improved while the cost of production went down.

Factories became even more productive when assembly lines further-reduced skilled work to the tedium of machine tending or putting on the another part in the eighteen seconds before the next unit came down the line. And again, production efficiency and standardization went up while automation caused the cost of production to plummet.

Electricity was a "general purpose" game-changing technology. When electricity came in, you could be out of a job, especially if you didn't want to get good at doing things the new way. Now, computers are also a new general-purpose technology. Once again, we are engaged in reinventing the work we do, how we organize our businesses, and how we manage our economy.

Since the early 1800s, growing productivity from increasing automation has caused the Gross Domestic Product (GDP) per person in America to keep on expanding. Worldwide growth has increased even faster. The key to this growth is combining our ability to apply knowledge creatively with our ability to make goods really fast.

But, in the end, those who finance the production are, more and more, the primary beneficiaries of these increased efficiencies. True, products may cost less, but fewer workers are working and they earn less for their labors.

Work has become a buyer's market. In fact, many people's wages are so low that they find they must swallow their pride and depend on government support programs just to manage. That is, the government has been drawn into using our taxes to supplement the poor wages and often-nonexistent benefits offered by many large corporations. I'll be spending several articles brooding on the related subject of jobs, work, living wages and income disparity. Please stay tuned.

Jobs: Part 2: Disintermediation

Whatever happened to all the travel agents, filling station attendants, and encyclopedia salesmen? It turns out they were middlemen – intermediaries between you and what you wanted. Therefore, you can say that, when we found ways to do their jobs more directly, they were "disintermediated."

These days, it is ever-more-common to "cut out the middleman." You book your own travel, pump your own gas, and easily search for information about any subject that interests you by using Internet search engines. The *Encyclopedia Britannica* has stopped printing paper volumes. Voluntary curators and editors contribute articles to Wikipedia, a free on-line encyclopedia with an increasingly solid reputation. Tesla Motors is working toward their vision of bypassing dealerships to sell electric automobiles directly to the public.

Businesses are increasingly likely to buy directly from manufacturers rather than using distributors, wholesalers, brokers, jobbers or agents. Many private individuals also exercise the growing opportunity to shop on the Internet and have their purchases shipped directly from the seller to their home. Fewer people are hired to stock shelves locally or show you their department's wares in person.

Even a business' own warehouses are often contracted to massive, highly automated, "order fulfillment" services. Outsourcing cuts out more jobs than you may think. The ideal product company now may have fewer than a dozen employees. They hire outside engineering and design services; they contract-out manufacturing; products are transported on container transport ships directly to a fulfillment partner. The company's home office may never see their actual products, except as samples sitting on the window ledge.

I worked in industry when the first experiments in Business-to-Business (B2B) private electronic networks were invented. By agreeing to terms and linking their computers, businesses could treat each other like their own specialty departments. Now, as described above,

Business-to-Consumer (B2C) organizations can eliminate wholesalers and retailers.

Individuals now have the ability to build products in their home and then sell them internationally. My wife likes to make colorful cloth covers for kitchen counter-top mixers. She can make anything that appeals to her and find a buyer on eBay or Etsy. She does not need to maintain a high volume, warehouse or sales force and has even had complete strangers ask her to do custom work. Maybe the old-fashioned craftsmen, cobblers, tinkers and tailors are coming back.

Like many modern authors and musicians, I have been able to publish my books directly to the public without an agent or outside publisher. My books are downloaded directly or printed by highly automated machines, one at a time, as they are ordered. On the one hand, I have to do all of the editing, layout, cover art and promotion myself. On the other hand, I get to keep the lion's share of royalties that are generated. Instead of teams of sales agents, I depend on word-of-mouth by friends and recommendations by satisfied readers on their social networks.

Disintermediation is a mixed blessing. Some jobs go away; some jobs are created. Everything costs less in the end. New opportunities open up for people willing to invest the effort to change with the times. This is the historically normal and natural course of progress.

Forgiveness of Debt

Jesus Christ taught his disciples to pray for forgiveness as they forgave others. Various translators have given this injunction as forgiveness of "trespasses," "sins," or "debts." While we can speculate endlessly about how such Christian forgiveness should work out in practice, the sense of the idea reflects a certain recurring traditional social contract. When we owe something, we should attend to repaying it. Further, it is wrong to expect leniency if we ourselves are impatient and demanding. However, individuals should not be reduced to intractable permanent poverty.

Many cultures institutionalize forgiveness of both moral and economic debts. For instance, the Law of Moses to the Jews directed that there be a periodic "Jubilee" year in which certain debts were to be forgiven. This has been described was "...a self-regulating system that deleveraged itself before credit bubbles grew out of control..." Also, the Koran holds a similar instruction that "... if (the debtor) is in [serious straits], then let there be postponement until (he is in) ease ... and that you remit it as alms is better for you..." For what it's worth, the Jubilee law even prescribed that farm land be given a rest every seven years so that it had a chance to recover and restore productivity.

Many people were aware of the "Occupy Wall Street" (OWS) protests at their peak, but now think that the movement has disappeared. Actually, it only got quieter while it organized a variety of initiatives. OWS volunteers were some of the most active responders in the aftermath of Hurricane Sandy.

One of the many OWS projects is "Rolling Jubilee," which uses donated funds to buy-up private debt (such as college loans) for pennies on the dollar – like collection agencies do. But, instead of hounding the debtor, it forgives the debt. In just their first month, they raised $474,723 to abolish $9,499,377 as an act of "mutual support and good will in pursuit of a new world based on common good, not Wall Street profits."

Today, many people find themselves in increasingly difficult and overwhelming circumstances. Without adequate health insurance, serious illnesses in families account for 60% of personal bankruptcies. Situations such as ballooning mortgages, being laid off, or college loans without having a living-wage job, can be devastating as well. We don't have to overspend to land in this kind of debt. The working poor and middle class have faced decades of degenerating economic headwinds (including fewer and poorer jobs) while bankers and corporations win increasing legislative favors and record profits.

OWS is not the only group that views modern investment banks and nonbank financial companies as increasingly predatory – using deceptive and abusive practices. That is why the Obama administration formed the Consumer Financial Protection Bureau and nominated Elizabeth Warren to be its head. The CFPB began overseeing debt collection agencies (including $850 billion in student loans) at the start of 2013.

Frankly, our national economy is currently "awash in unpayable debt." Financial institutions are already sometimes obliged to "take a haircut" by canceling a portion of each other's debt. International banks have allowed entire countries to recover their economies through debt forgiveness. We will be seeing a growing national conversation develop about the possible benefits of consumer debt relief.

How to Save the World

In my family, both of my parents are dying and my grandchildren are about to inherit the earth. Dad spent many years on an assembly line making cars. I worked at refineries making gasoline. He enjoyed traveling and drove to California 23 times, just for starters. I live in a very small rural town and don't think twice about driving 60 miles round trip just for a special supper out. Have we made it more unlikely that our children's children will have a world worth inheriting?

Thinking about the many issues of ecology and economics makes my head want to explode. Nevertheless, somehow, it still seems important enough to try to wrap my mind around it. If not for me, than for the ones I love. It turns out that smart people of good will are actually starting to get a handle on all of this. Some scientists are focusing on barely-imaginable details. Other researchers are backing off far enough to get an overall picture of the entire forest of environmental and social issues.

Surely, it is obvious that our finite world cannot sustain infinite growth. We must discover, meet and deal with limits to growth. Yet, we continue to expect that every nation's Gross Domestic Product (GDP) must always continue to grow to provide improving standards of living for a growing percent of our populations. Something has to give. We need to maximize security and quality of life without excessively depleting the resources we depend on to sustain that life.

Our societies also have certain minimum economic and social expectations. The list may include good health, accessible and nutritious food, available clean water, equitable personal income, universal access to education, strength of our institutions, opportunities for personal expression, satisfying and sustaining work, available and affordable energy, and broad social equalities. Without these societal benefits, we are unhappy and feel insecure.

On the other hand, our environment has certain maximum limits that are being challenged. Without effectively managing our consumption of resources, we're all doomed to face disaster. We have to solve problems of freshwater use, agricultural methods, ocean acidification, pollution, aerosols and particles in the air, ozone depletion, buildup of methane and carbon dioxide producing climate change, loss of biodiversity, deforestation and weapons of mass destruction.

Each of these issues represents a compelling need or threat. But, trade-offs between our minimums and maximums are available if we summon the collective will to make the effort. There is a middle area, like the circle of a donut, that forms a "safe and just space for humanity." We need to keep working on balances and compromises in order to hit, and stay within, that sweet spot.

It's likely that many of our children will suffer terribly before we decide that survival will require major changes. The more of us that accept that fact, and the sooner we commit to needed change, the less long-term damage will accrue. Our issues of satisfaction are no longer just personal or community problems; our survival requires us to think and act as a species.

Perhaps there is hope that the world will not end… yet. To learn more, try a web search for "A Safe and Just Space for Humanity." What will our children's children inherit?

Delayed Recovery from Climate Change Gasses

Dear Editor,

Your Editorial opinion (*Messenger News*, Feb. 17, 2012) about coal, gas emissions, and global warming seems to be misinformed. You referred to a new article in *Science* to oppose "Obama's EPA." You also stated that the American people have been misled and that Congress should be furious with [President] Obama.

I looked up the research report and found that CO_2 emissions are still important because they produce "long-term inertial responses." One conclusion, however, was that efforts to reduce emissions of methane and soot (which act more quickly) should receive additional priorities in order achieve greater short-term benefits.

Also, it seems that coal mining releases methane and burning coal emits soot. Therefore, your argument against the actions of our government to protect our welfare is weakened. I also came across information that the health costs related to burning coal is approximately equal to the value of the energy produced.

I, for one, am glad that research is already reducing production costs for systems such as the wind generators that help make Iowa a net exporter of energy.

David Satterlee

This morning, I opened the *Fort Dodge Messenger News*, my local daily newspaper. I've been skipping past the editorial section because it tends to feature mostly conservative columnists beating the same old drums. Today, feeling the sap rising in the grass-roots democratic arm of the Democratic Party, I decided to start reading the paper regularly.

The publisher's editorial was featured in a top outside corner. It was an uninformed rant about President Barack Obama, and how "his EPA" should be stopped by a furious Congress. As I started to turn the page, yet again, I felt a flush of heat that so many readers were being led down the wrong path; that an editor was improperly echoing the inflammatory language and rants of conservative pseudo-authorities to lie to people who have been primed to accept the word of their authorities.

As an aging hippie, I was raised to "question authority," so I decided to get back in the game. Here it is. Please read on. We'll start with the full text of the editorial:

> Have we been misled? [Publisher's Editorial]
> February 17, 2012
> *Messenger News* [Fort Dodge, Iowa, USA]
>
> "The science is settled," President Barack Obama insists in defense of his scheme to wreck the coal industry.
>
> Well, no. It is not.
>
> Obama insists the threat of global warming requires drastic new curbs on industrial emissions. Coal-burning power plants have been a primary target of the Environmental Protection Agency.
>
> Unless discharges of carbon dioxide into the air are reduced dramatically, the planet faces severe changes in climate, Obama, the EPA and supportive liberals have maintained.
>
> A new study on the issue is out. It has been published in the online journal "Science."
>
> And guess what?
>
> The international team of scientists involved in the study concludes cutting emissions of soot and methane - not CO^2 - is the key to slowing global warming.
>
> That is hardly settled science.

Members of Congress, who have the power to stop Obama and his EPA, should be furious. Clearly, they and the American people have been misled.

Okay, so here's where I'm going with my argument. [*The number of each summary comment corresponds with a more-detailed comment to follow. Also, the extended comments are somewhat out of order because I thought it improved the clarity of a linear reading.*]

1. Ha! By highlighting some gasses that contribute to global warming over others, the editor may have accidently conceded the issue of global warming.
2. The scientific study does NOT actually discount CO^2 as a major greenhouse gas.
3. The science on methane and soot is hardly new.
4. Coal fired power plants are, themselves, major contributors to methane and soot.
5. The EPA is also already concerned about methane and soot.
6. President Obama is not pursuing a scheme to "wreck the coal industry" so much as to increase our energy resources, make our air and water cleaner and, commendably, help save the world.
7. This kind of misinformation is bad for America. The editor should think more carefully. We should work to improve the functions of government in areas where government is best suited to helping make our lives better.
8. We should each work to become better informed, more involved in civic discourse, and supportive of leaders who are committed to the goal of making the lives of individual citizens better.
9. The argument that the United States should fight to keep up with developing countries in the emission of pollutants because it is more *profitable*, is simply less *honorable*.

1) Many conservative commentators continue to use words such as myth, swindle, and hoax to describe the results of climate science research. I am afraid these simple negative messages, repeated

frequently, are taken by many as persuasive and factual. Not wanting to be carried along blindly by that agenda, I looked up the actual study.

2) The editorial alludes to, but does not cite, the article "Simultaneously Mitigating Near-Term Climate Change and Improving Human Health and Food Security" on pages 183-189 of the January 13, 2012 issue of *Science*.

The authors took advantage of continuing research to create a detailed computer model of our atmosphere's response to pollutants and (for the first time) possible economic, energy generation, social, political and developmental influences. However, it does not yet make predictions for major societal shifts such as switching to electric vehicles or increased levels of public transportation. The research is available online at http://gains.iiasa.ac.at The research is designed to support international negotiations and strategy coordination.

The study points out that CO_2 emissions produce "long-term inertial responses" but that reducing soot and methane emissions is more likely to produce short-term benefits. This does not affect the understanding of the effect of CO_2 on global warming; it just adds more urgency to our priorities in also addressing soot and methane reductions.

5) Fortunately, the Environmental Protection Agency (EPA) is already on top of this situation with projects such as those to reduce methane released by coal mining and soot released by burning coal in electrical power generating plants. Dang, the editor must have overlooked these pollutants as additional results of burning coal.

3) Our understanding of the influences on global climate change has included soot and methane for years. The same *Science* journal has already published related articles including, "Soot Takes Center Stage" (Sept. 27, 2002), and "Study Fingers Soot as a Major Player in Global Warming" (Mar. 28, 2008). The Nov. 10, 2000 article "A New Route Toward Limiting Climate Change?" explored short-term pollutants such as soot.

4) Coal fired power plants do more than emit CO^2. It seems they are a major source of other greenhouse gasses as well. Generating electricity from coal also emits more arsenic, mercury and lead than any other U.S. industrial pollution source. According to a Chesapeake Bay Foundation report, "A Coal Plant's Drain on Health and Wealth," the health costs of coal power plants are estimated to be equal to the price of the electricity they produce. (This sucker is already getting too long, so let's move on.)

6) Yeah. So there. Take that. The balanced liberal approach is to gradually retire the worst of the coal power plants, add pollution controls to the rest, and promote research and development of alternatives. This is clearly in the public interest. However, companies in the energy generation business have little incentive to make changes until the costs of a crisis exceed the costs of a new technology. By then, everyone will be wringing their hands and wondering why nobody thought to look into making alternatives more price-competitive.

By the way, while our use of coal can be improved, why do I keep hearing the term "clean coal" like someone has discovered a completely new thing, blessed it with holy water and invested in infomercials? Okay, now I'm just getting cranky.

7) This kind of editorial misinformation is bad for America. The editor should take care to be better informed, such as actually reading his source material. We should work to improve the functions of government in areas where government is best suited to helping make our lives better.

8) We should each work to become better informed. We all benefit by being more involved in civic discourse and supporting leaders who are committed to the goal of improving the lives of individual citizens.

9) The United States of America began with the blessing of a vast, resource-laden, productive, unexploited continent at its disposal. Much of America's success in the era of industrialization can be attributed to an "aggressive pioneer spirit." That disposition moved us inexorably

west, killing wantonly, cutting trees, setting fences, building roads, plowing fields and leveling mountains as we went. Our fertile fields, open waterways and abundant minerals rewarded new settlers with relatively easy wealth to harvest. Profits from exploiting this natural abundance were even greater for the privileged robber barons, industrialists and financiers.

Unbridled exploitation and consumption worked well for several hundred years. I can understand why some people want to be allowed to continue taking, wasting and polluting however they want just like they have been doing so far. However, we are reaching the limits of our clear vistas, standing timber, open prairies and clean rivers bounding from unexplored wilderness. It is time to be conservative – protecting, defending and wisely using what remains of our resources.

And, by the way, if it is primarily liberals petitioning for moderation, caution, and conservation, what has happened to the meaning of the word "conserve"ative?

Precision Farming Reboot - A new paradigm using sensors, robots and lasers

As my wife and I drove down a rural Iowa highway last week, we began speculating about the next revolution in field management. Currently, tractors blindly and mechanically groom rows of crops spaced only wide enough to accommodate their massive tires. Large quantities of herbicides and insecticides are broadcast, leaching into streams and aquifers. In turn, specially bred seeds, resistant to these chemicals must be purchased as a part of a proprietary program.

Instead, I imagined swarms of spider-shaped robots with travel legs long enough to keep their body suspended above the crops. Work arms, tipped with sensors and tools, could maneuver to any spot.

- Plants could be grown in an efficient honeycomb pattern, wasting less space.
- A database of every plant, with its progress, could be maintained.
- Instead of making care decisions on a whole-field basis, adaptive algorithms could adjust interventions for increasingly small or divergent areas.
- Micro-doses of fertilizer/nutrients could be injected under the surface, sufficient for each plant without over-spray or windblown residue.
- Individual weed plants could be identified and selectively uprooted or destroyed.
- Individual bugs could be identified and selectively destroyed.
- Individual bugs could be harvested using a suction device. Some bugs contain valuable chemicals such as dyes or pharmaceutical components.
- Crop plants could be automatically thinned or even transplanted to more-sparse areas of a field.
- Robots could work continuously, even at night, returning to an energy source to recharge or exchange batteries when necessary.

- Some labor-intensive jobs, such as harvesting strawberries, currently require large amounts of manual labor for brief periods. Machines would be easier to store and transport from place to place than seasonal workers.

The next day, I discovered that researchers at Leibniz University in Germany are exploring how to use lasers to kill weeds. Cameras feed pattern-recognition software to identify weed plants and distinguish them from the crop plants. Tunable lasers aim at the most vulnerable areas of weeds, to kill them. During their experimental trials, the German researchers found that lesser intensities of laser light actually stimulated plant development. This discovery raises the potential for non-chemical stimulation of crop growth.

Researchers in Israel are developing multi-spectral sensors for identifying fruits and vegetables along with their stages of ripeness. These systems are already able to correctly identify 80-85 percent of fruit on a plant. They are also designing grasping tools that can remove individual pieces without damaging them or the remaining plant.

This is a field (pun intended) to keep your eye on. The core issue of agricultural productivity has always been the limitations of manpower. Perhaps it is time to look away from ever-larger mega-machines. These mini-factories-on-wheels are becoming highly automated themselves, in any event. An agricultural technology revolution is afoot.

Further, we are beginning to recognize the shortsightedness of consuming large quantities of just a few single vitamin- and mineral-deficient crops (wheat and corn, especially) while depending on ever-stronger pesticides and herbicides and ever-larger machines.

Our future will be a place for increasingly smarter and more-flexible machines. The next step is to teach highly automated machines to perform the tedious judgment-intense precision farm work that we can no longer afford to do in person.

How I got from There to Here

[Catching up with an old friend from high school.]

Dear Bob,

Damn, it's been more than a year since I finally found you on the Internet, and what do I do after decades of regularly wondering "whatever became of…?" I drop the ball. Thank you for your reply via Facebook message. It was short enough to be modest and long enough to open the door to seriously catching up. I'll start by replying to it.

You may remember that, in high school, I had precious few friends, that I was socially reclusive, and that my religion seemed to be against almost everything. Fair enough. Somehow, you found it in yourself to be kind to me and I still count you (other than the two women I've married) as my second and last "best friend." So, that means a lot to me, but enough with weeping and gnashing teeth.

Memorizing 100 digits of pi? The way I remember it, I discovered that, as with trying to memorize "The Ride of Lochinvar," I have an exceptionally poor memory for raw detail. You mastered that beast to about 130 places while I struggled to retain about 20 digits. I learned to pick my contests more judiciously. I'm still good for 3.14159, which seems adequate for most purposes. OMG, it just came back: You used to joke that: "Pie are not square. Cornbread are square. Pie are round!"

No, I'm no longer one of Jehovah's Witnesses. Even in school, I was struggling with some issues of faith. In 1972, I married Debbie from Springfield, Missouri. She and her mother converted within a year of each other while Debbie was in college. She was a devout believer and together we raised two boys as active JWs. We almost got them grown and out of the house before they bailed on the faith. On the other hand, I kept struggling to make everything work out until I blew out the whole thing. Debbie and I were ill suited. She was raised by a hard driving career Army officer and didn't hesitate to butt heads. I never figured out, in 27 years of marriage, how to make her happy with herself or with me.

I have a theory about depression being a natural result when the self becomes exhausted in battling intractable issues. By about 1994, I was at odds with my family, my church, my job and myself. The medical psychiatrist I saw prescribed drugs, which I judged brought me from about 15% functionality to about 35%. I was probably being optimistic; I hit just about every indicator for diagnosis of depression except attempted suicide, although I had recurring urges to swerve my car under the trailer wheels of big trucks and started making inventories of unguarded concrete pillars. It truly called to me, but I was too stubborn to do it; there is always hope for change.

I picked up the advice somewhere: "If your behaviors are contrary to your values, pick one and change the other." And, so I did. In 1998, the boys were grown up and moved out and I bailed too. I left my home, my religion, and my work. My stated intent was to stop being a burden, recover and then return. (Nobody claims that I was thinking rationally.)

As it turned out, I quickly discovered that Debbie was determined to stay rid of me. It was the start of my recovery. I discovered immense relief from the mental burdens I had been holding onto. She filed for divorce several years later and we hardly communicate with each other yet.

On the bright side, my sister eventually convinced me to put my profile up on Match.com and see about "meeting a nice lady." It wasn't a very good idea at first. Most women quickly identified me as an unemployable basket case. I was surprised when Dianna, from 200 miles away, sent me a "wink." She saw something intriguing and appealing about my self-description. We visited about four times before we decided to marry, which we did within another two weeks. We agree that if any of our children had pulled such a stunt, we would certainly have condemned their haste and threatened to lock them in a closet.

Dianna and I continue to love and adore each other. She thinks I'm the kindest person she's ever met and I admire her character and love her great and empathetic heart. I'm still socially reclusive but she has me back in harness and on the path. In short, we're as comfortable with each other as two puppies in a basket.

Okay, back to high school and my career path. As a "good JW youth," I rejected higher education. I believed, as I had been taught, that it would only raise questions and lead me away from the faith. In retrospect that would have been more desirable than less, but we sometimes have to learn these things the hard way.

So, I got a job as a stock handler at Hallmark Cards' Liberty distribution warehouse. I contracted a dreadful case of infectious hepatitis and was admitted to Smithville hospital two days after Debbie and I were married. I was as weak as a new kitten for weeks and, from then on, required about ten hours of sleep each night. (That didn't get us off to a good start.)

I was able to bid into a technical job doing first-response maintenance on Hallmark's twelve mobile warehousing elevators. These things were computer-controlled (in 1969!) and ran down towering storage aisles on railroad tracks while also moving a forklift platform vertically. Upon arriving, they stored or retrieved a pallet of goods and returned to an automated set of roller conveyers. The job was a hoot. I did it well and was taking the initiative to study the control schematics in hopes of advancing to a full electronics maintenance position.

But, being a good JW, when the warehouse went on rotating shifts and I discovered that I would miss congregation meetings on a regular basis. I gave up what promised to be a stable job and fascinating career and moved the two of us to Marshall, Missouri, where we rented half of an old house for $65/month and I opened a CB radio repair shop in the back of a well-known CB store. Leaving Hallmark for self-employment was a bad idea, and not just in retrospect. We had no money, and most of the money we didn't have had to go into the business. Debbie took a job in the PR department of the local college.

One night, in a fit of uncharacteristic loss of caution, we started our first boy. After a few months of growing recognition of the consequences, I took a full-time job repairing televisions (and helping to deliver appliances) for a local appliance store. After another few months of growing recognition, I realized that the other guy always gave me the heavy compressor end of air conditioners to carry. But, I digress.

Determined to better our situation that spring, I selected six towns where we thought we might like to live, and sent out resume letters to 50 businesses. Curiously, this actually resulted in two sight-unseen job offers. I took the one from Cheyenne, Wyoming and began repairing commercial two-way radios and helping to raise antenna towers. They had a contract that summer to install a 50-location emergency medical radio system in the southern part of the state. I got to do things like crawl on top of a $75,000 Cadillac ambulance, sight down the middle and drill a ¾" antenna hole in the roof.

We also maintained repeater towers in places like Cheyenne Peak. I went up that mountain once in a helicopter and once up the rocky backside in show shoes. However, come Christmas time, the business slowed down and the new guy had to go. By now, our boy was toddling and we had enough money (only if we sold the car) to pay another month's rent (in the middle of winter in an isolated corner of Wyoming) or rent a U-Haul and move in on my parents in Liberty while I looked for work around Kansas City.

I managed to land a great job at DIT-MCO near Central Park. They used be the "Drive In Theatre Manufacturing Company" but they invented the technology for an automated wiring analyzer. They suddenly became vital to the aerospace and electronic circuit manufacturing industries. I got plopped down in the middle of the final-assembly quality assurance test department. It was a sink-or-swim environment. Fortunately, I was in the habit of self-directed learning and floated to the top.

The machines were essentially glorified ohmmeters except that:

1. they used up to 5 amps for very low resistance tests and up to 1500 volts for very high resistance tests,
2. instead of two probe wires, they could have up to thousands of relay-switched wires that would be run to every wire termination in an aircraft, space capsule, or electronic assembly, and
3. the system could examine a known-good sample under computer control and then use that information to rapidly test other parts to verify intended connections and assure no unintended connections. It then printed an exception list for needed repairs.

I was promoted to an engineering assistant and was assigned to build custom and prototype systems. I was also put in charge of metrology standards for a NBS-traceable calibration program. It was a great work environment but, although they were generous with learning-curve time, they were tight with wages.

I applied at other places. The electric shop at the Amoco Refinery in Sugar Creek (just north of Independence) would have doubled my wages, but they didn't invite me for an interview.

However, ElectroDynamics, just over the Kansas line, needed a go-getter maintenance engineer. They manufactured quartz oscillating crystals – mostly to keep time in digital clocks and set oscillator frequencies in radios and televisions. This was another great job. I worked with their full range of manufacturing equipment. They grew large, uniform quartz crystals in converted cannon barrels and then sliced, shaped, and ground the quartz wafers. They sputtered silver electrodes onto the surfaces under high vacuum, tuned them in baths of iodine vapors, precision-welded them into miniature cans, and tested for leaks in liquid-nitrogen cooled spectrophotometers. It felt like glory days.

Then, Amoco called and offered me impossibly high wages; primarily to repair their 2-way radio systems. In my time there, I also learned pneumatic, hydraulic, electro-mechanical, and digital process control systems. I came in as a journeyman electrician in the Oil, Chemical & Atomic Workers Union. I would install or repair darn near anything. I might go from replacing a miniaturized resister three components deep inside a radio to wiring a massive 1200-volt 3-phase motor, to polishing the drive take-off plates of a locomotive, to calibrating an analytical instrument in the lab.

My peers called me "Two-Gun" because I wore carefully packed twin tool pouches when I left the central shop. I was loaded for bear. Then, the warehouse installed an inventory computer; I was the only one interested in learning how to wire-up the terminals and their digital networking interfaces. Oh, and I also joined the refinery and City of Liberty volunteer fire departments.

And then, Amoco closed Sugar Creek. I was offered a place in the electrical department in Whiting, Indiana, but it would have been a dead end job in a miserable town. I found a job advertisement in the *Houston Post* for a salaried job in Amoco's Texas City computerized process control engineering department. I applied outside of the take-it-or-leave-it transfer system and landed the position; getting a salaried-employee's moving bonus in the process.

In seventeen years at Texas City, I worked with three generations of plant-wide data acquisition systems. One of my first jobs was to take $750,000 (this is in 1978 dollars) of newly appropriated capital funds and invent a new system from scratch. They must have been desperate to give a new-to-the-plant, non-degreed, un-tested bloke project management and engineering responsibilities. Nonetheless, I worked hard, pulled some inventive stunts and got the job done. I wrote and helped present a paper on it for the National Petroleum Refiner's Association's annual conference in New Orleans.

My last data acquisition system was the largest of its kind in the world, monitoring and archiving over 50,000 temperatures, pressures, flows, and levels at 6-second to 1-minute intervals. I ended up as the Systems Manager for this network of DEC VAX computers. In the meantime, I did database programming on an IBM VM mainframe, helped start-up a computer and PC support group/helpdesk, organize and present computer classes to the refinery's engineers, served as Chairman of the Refinery Communication Committee, and introduced their first refinery-wide network for computer and video. Everybody started calling me "Computer Dave."

I got pissed when, after several years of prime yearly appraisals and no promotion, a supervisor confessed that they had to throttle my advancement to accommodate "career potential." I immediately understood that they would never formally put someone with nothing but high school, self-study and moxie into a supervisory role over chemical, electrical and mechanical engineers from Purdue. I stayed pissed. Having already peaked in the best (and best-paying) job I could ever hope to get, I developed an interest in herbalism and redirected my interests. I decided to become "a nationally-known natural health educator" within ten years.

At about this time, the oil industry was being squeezed financially; international exploration projects were costing a mint and turning out badly. We started belt-tightening like everybody else. There was no money for important maintenance, training or even money-saving projects that previously would have been no-brainers. The culture in the technical departments degenerated from we-all-work-together to don't-talk-to-me-without-a-charge-code. I was more than pissed; I was disillusioned.

When a voluntary retirement downsizing offer hit our department, I signed up. I decided to open a supplement store and become an herbalist. And, become an herbalist, I did – doing a lot of good for a lot of people.

However, like my CB radio shop, this was stupid on a grand scale. It didn't help that I was becoming severely diabetic and didn't even realize it until 1997, when my peripheral neuropathy was raging fire and needles. This development was really embarrassing; "herbalist heal thyself."

I was thoroughly consumed by depression by this time, but I hired good help. Eventually Debbie (sorry, she insisted on being called Deborah by this time) left her hair pulling job as a legal secretary (for a man I believed to be an alcoholic stress-jockey) and became the store manager and bookkeeper. This allowed me to retire to the back room for the self-study, customer consultations and writing I could still manage.

One of the things I wrote was an index card set explaining the rational for the medicinal uses of individual herbs and standard formulations. I eventually sold 38,000 copies of this self-published work, along with subscriptions to semi-annual updates. For about 5 years, it was *the* go-to reference in its niche. I also wrote freelance articles for journals such as *Nature's Field* and related educational newsletters.

At the store, I had a $2000/year library budget and used it to build a reference collection that spanned six bookcases and a clipping file that filled 3 file cabinets. I was determined to find the best evidence-based resources. I leveraged this into HerbalDave.com and sold a CD version of the web site that contained over 10,000 linked pages. I actually got good in the field and endorsed complementary therapies that American MDs are only starting to recommend over a decade later.

I was asked to join an advisory committee for a new elective on CAM [Complementary and Alternative Medicine] at UTMB [University of Texas Medical Branch]. The instructor asked me to become a community proctor for Juniors and Seniors taking that elective. His medical students typically spent the better part of a full day with me, one-on-one, at some time during the semester.

However, my depression deepened and I struggled to remain functional. If you have had patients tell you how hard it is to find the motivation to roll over in bed, to say nothing of climbing out of the pit to do something useful, I will testify that it is real. Eventually, Deborah had to ban me from the store. I had started getting testy with perfectly good customers and locking the door if someone threw a cigarette butt on the sidewalk on their way in. I only got to come in to teach some night classes and for paid personal consultations. The 10-week group-study series based on Joseph Pizzorno's *Total Wellness* had to be repeated for a waiting list. I managed to finish it, but that was about all I could do in public for the balance of the week, for 20 weeks.

As already mentioned, I eventually concluded that I must leave or die; I cut my family, spiritual and business ties and moved out of state. I was bound for Brevard, North Carolina where I was convinced that an herbal manufacturing company could not function without me. I found a part-time job as a clerk in a little health food store while I laid siege to every help-wanted ad that the herb company posted. The owner's executive secretary eventually sent word that I was making him crazy and would I please cut it out.

I also set up a business as an Amazon.com used book vendor. I specialized in hardback nonfiction that I foraged at Goodwill stores, friend of library sales, and such. It was a tidy little business that I could work at my own pace and quite alone. I set up my computer to play a cash register "ka-ching" noise when an order came through; it always brightened the moment.

I was still writing freelance articles for magazines including one published by leading herbalist. When I heard that his senior editor was moving on, I was already known there as his "most outstanding (correspondence) student," a writer whose "articles don't have to be rewritten," and the author of "that reference card set." I called and he hired me on the phone. I packed everything that would fit in my Ford Aspire hatchback and moved to Utah. I lived on his couch for 3 weeks and in my car in the office parking lot for three more before finding a small rental trailer.

This herbalist is a gifted teacher. He is emotionally open and his audiences love him for his sincerity, enthusiasm and passion. He writes rapidly from experience, can record a flawless hour-long video presentation without rehearsal or hesitation … and needed an editor.

On the other hand, he wanted to commit to every clever idea he had – I became responsible for herding much of it to completion on tight deadlines. He also had a fragile ego and a girlfriend who would regularly reduce him to tears. I was slower and more deliberate, but we were a pretty good match.

However, after a year and a half together, he overextended himself developing a private supplement product line and keeping too many irons in the fire. He ran out of payroll money and tightened-up the business. With fewer irons in the fire, he had the time to resume the work I had been doing for him. It probably didn't help that I had begun suggesting substantive edits to some of his first drafts.

Curiously, the timing was perfect. My aged parents called and told me that my 87-year old Uncle Ed was recovering in the hospital from hip replacement surgery and wanted to return to his home in Excelsior Springs. Mom said straight out, "we need you here." For another year and a half, I was Ed's in-home primary care-giver. Almost every day, we visited his wife in a nearby nursing home dementia wing.

I appropriated Ed's basement and started an eBay business reselling items I acquired at local auctions. One of my best short stories progressively reveals the difficulty and repetitive nature of elder care (and Ed's devotion to his beloved Jessie). Of the first few people to seen it; they all cried. [Read it in *Life Will Get You in the End*, "Going to See Jessie."]

I was still taking care of Uncle Ed when I met and married Dianna, an elementary school teacher. Di and I lived apart for a while, trying to figure out the best way to reconcile our individual responsibilities. She had just moved to teach in a 1-school rural district. It was looking like a bad decision. We decided to move her from Russell, Iowa to join me in Excelsior Springs. But first, we agreed to drive a U-Haul with my sister's furniture from Lenexa, Kansas to Los Angeles. While we were gone, my mother admitted Ed to a hospital for a relatively minor complaint. He was discharged to a nursing home and never got out. So, I moved to Iowa instead and took up residence with my new wife.

We finished the teaching year but discovered that the school would be closed soon [it struggled through one more year]. Deciding that we had the opportunity to live anywhere we chose, she sent resumes to several counties in the Appalachian mountains of Western North Carolina. Di is truly an outstanding teacher and was hired at her first interview. She taught for five years in an area with highly subsidized school lunch programs; it was poor and rural with many remote mountain families. Directly adjacent to Cherokee and the Qualla Boundary, Dianna was requested by name by many tribal parents. I became the househusband and supported her work at every opportunity.

After five years, a new principal, adverse to her "unconventional (creative but effective), tree-hugging liberal ways," bluntly asserting, "I can buy two fresh graduates for what I'm paying you." We were convinced that it was time for Di to retire. This meant that we could not afford to stay in our beloved hole-in-the-woods mountain home. We hired a management company and rented it out until it sold. I found a solid but neglected house in Iowa, just 12 miles from a set of grandchildren who needed our support.

My spiritual transformations continue to be a work in progress. I have read extensively about Buddhism and spent a lot of time studying the work of Ken Wilber and other developmental theorists. In a succession of worldviews I have believed that: God was always watching and fearsome, obedience was required to gain approval, I must work hard to achieve advancement, I must contribute to community and harmony, the diverse streams of action and knowledge can be understood and mastered, and row-row-row-your-boat-gently-down-the-stream.

It seems that the essence of morality ("goodness") is the use of intelligence, energy and love to create. For instance, creating a garden path, butter churn, or piece of art is good; vandalism of a creative work is bad.

It seems like there may be a universal pool of consciousness from which we spring like drops and into which we return.

Perhaps acts of living contribute to a common memory so things that have happened increase the probability that they will happen again.

Perhaps continuous interactions of energy and events guarantee that unlikely events will continuously arise and generate new possibilities.

Perhaps some great cause unrolled itself into the chaotic plasma of everything-yet-nothing-in-particular and the whole mess is in the process of rolling itself back into a coherent unity of oneness.

It seems that the purpose of life is to contribute to the increasing sustainability, diversity, complexity and organization of life… sentience… consciousness.

It seems that we must "be the good that we want to see," and commit to helping all sentient beings to develop toward greater goodness.

Best wishes and fondest regards,

DavidS

[*My lengthy piece, "Honoring My Father" is a natural fit to extend my autobiographical history. However, I have already published it separately. Dianna has persuaded me to not duplicate it here at the risk of irritating readers when they discover that they have purchased it twice. It is a memorium to the goodness in my Father's life and an ironic take on the circumstances of a dysfunctional funeral. Naturally, I think it is a good read and recommend it to you.*]

Gratitude to the Reader – and a Request

You are a vital part of marketing for a new generation of self-published authors. *Thank you for buying and reading this book!* If you would be so kind, please let others know that they should read it and why you recommend it. This is how much of publishing works now. Thank you, thank you, thank you.

This book was self-published using the resources of CreateSpace. It could not have been completed and marketed without modern web-based technology and this old fart loves tech. Thank you to all the optimistic techies out there. Have you hugged your nerd today?

Special thanks to Dianna Satterlee, my wife. Di is a bright soul, the light of my heart, a retired teacher, gifted cook and special friend. She has made the lives of many, many people better for her being in this world. She is also the secret sauce in my recipe for writing, and has inspired, cooperated, facilitated and participated in many ways.

You should know that I also write short fiction. The stories are a nice change of pace and easier to digest than essays. I like tugging at your heartstrings or putting a gotcha twist at the end. Please look for them.

Follow me online at:

DavidSatterlee.com
@DavidSatterlee
@ChumForThought
SocioDynamics.org
www.facebook.com/david.satterlee

www.ingramcontent.com/pod-product-compliance
Lightning Source LLC
Chambersburg PA
CBHW070144290526
45789CB00002B/629